THE CONTEMPLATIVE WAY OF PRAYER

The Contemplative Way of Prayer

Deepening Your Life with God

Robert Faricy, S.J.
Lucy Rooney, S.N.D.

SERVANT BOOKS
Ann Arbor, Michigan

Published by Servant Books
P.O. Box 8617
Ann Arbor, Michigan 48107

88 89 90 91   10 9 8 7 6 5 4 3

Printed in the United States of America
ISBN 0-89283-308-4

Library of Congress Cataloging-in-Publication Data

Faricy, Robert L., 1926—
    The contemplative way of prayer.

    1. Prayer.   2. Pentecostalism.   3. Contemplation.
I. Rooney, Lucy.   II. Title.
BV210.2.F37   1986   248.3'4   86-15580
ISBN 0-89283-308-4

Contents

Preface

WE HAVE WRITTEN THIS BOOK TO HELP YOU enter into closer personal relationship with Jesus Christ through prayer. What we have written depends on the whole Christian tradition of prayer and, in particular, on two broad currents within Christianity. The first is the whole Catholic tradition of contemplative prayer. The second is the pentecostal current that, having begun in the pentecostal churches, has passed into all the major Christian churches.

The book is mainly for Christians who have some kind of charismatic experience. This includes, of course, many people who have never participated in charismatic or pentecostal groups, as well as all those who have.

We both pray that it helps you to come closer to the Lord in your prayer.

Lucy Rooney, S.N.D.
Robert Faricy, S.J.

ONE

The Charismatic Experience and Personal Prayer

THE "CHARISMATIC EXPERIENCE" is the experience of the power of the Holy Spirit in my life. The experience of the power of the Spirit of Jesus, whether I have that experience in or outside a charismatic or pentecostal group or church, is by its nature charismatic and pentecostal. It includes an outpouring of the gifts and charisms of the Spirit. And it shares in the outpouring of the Holy Spirit that began at the first Pentecost with the descent of the Spirit on the disciples of Jesus, gathered for prayer in the upper room in Jerusalem.

The experience of the power of the Spirit of Jesus is always a call to personal prayer, a call to enter more deeply into personal relationship with Jesus, an invitation. "Come to me, all you who labor and are burdened, and I will give you rest. Take my yoke upon you, and learn from me, for I am meek and humble of heart; and you will find rest for your souls" (Mt 11:28-29).

Baptism in the Holy Spirit, and After

Millions of Christians all over the world have received, in some form, the "baptism in the Holy Spirit." Perhaps most of these take part, or have taken part, in a charismatic renewal group or a pentecostal church. Many other Christians have received the baptism in the Holy Spirit—maybe without knowing what to call it—on their own, alone, not as a member of any particular pentecostal or charismatic group.

How can I understand the baptism in the Holy Spirit so that I can better see its meaning for personal prayer and especially for contemplative prayer? Why do so many people have a burst of prayer fervor after the baptism in the Holy Spirit and then, after a few weeks or some months, lose heart, pray less, fall off in enthusiasm for prayer and in the practice of prayer? What can they do?

The baptism in the Holy Spirit.
When we talk about the baptism in the Holy Spirit, we use the word *baptism* in an analogous sense. We do not mean baptism by water, the sacrament of Baptism. Baptism by water is a true sacrament—an outward sign that gives grace. The baptism in the

Holy Spirit is the Lord's response to prayer. We pray with someone that he or she will receive a new outpouring of the Holy Spirit; the Lord answers our prayer by pouring out his Spirit on the person we pray with.

The Lord, of course, gives his Spirit at the reception of the sacrament of Baptism. And he continues to pour out the Holy Spirit afterward. What then is so special about the "baptism in the Holy Spirit"?

The great medieval theologian St. Thomas Aquinas put it this way: The Lord always gives us his Spirit, as long as we stay in the Lord's grace. Grace, the grace that heals us interiorly and that helps us to grow in holiness, is precisely the effect of the Holy Spirit's presence in us.

The Holy Spirit himself is divine love, the mutual love between Jesus and the Father. When Jesus and the Father give me their Spirit, I find myself caught up in their love, in the divine love itself, and that love heals and makes holy.

Sometimes, quite rarely, I might receive an especially great grace, a grace that transforms my life, that converts me in a new way, a grace that I cannot doubt. I *know* God has touched me and radically changed me. We can speak of such a grace, says St. Thomas Aquinas, as a new sending of the Holy Spirit, as a new outpouring of the Holy Spirit.

In the charismatic renewal and in the pentecostal churches, we call the first of these unusually powerful and transforming outpourings of the Spirit, the baptism in the Holy Spirit. Can I receive the baptism in the Holy Spirit more than once? Not really. The Lord can give me other great graces that truly change my life in an extraordinary way. But only the first such grace is called the baptism in the Holy Spirit.

Do some people receive the baptism of the Holy Spirit outside any pentecostal or charismatic group? Yes, many, although they might not call it by that name. The Lord baptizes in his Spirit whom he wants to, when he wants to, and how he wants to. We know persons who have received such a first transforming outpouring of the Spirit during silent retreats. Others have received such a grace making the Spiritual Exercises of Ignatius of Loyola, not only in silent retreats but in everyday life. Others, during moments of quiet prayer, or in church, or at some totally unexpected moment.

The effects of the baptism in the Holy Spirit.
What does the baptism in the Holy Spirit do? When the Spirit comes in great abundance, overwhelmingly, the results may come to light immediately. The person can feel almost overcome by God's grace and completely changed right on the spot. Or it can take time. When I (Robert Faricy) received prayer for the baptism in the Spirit, apparently nothing happened; but, gradually, dramatic changes took place in my whole relationship with the Lord, in my

prayer, in my teaching and writing, in counseling others.

What happens? What happens, either more or less immediately, or at least gradually over a period of a few days or weeks or months, is this: The person the Lord baptizes in the Holy Spirit finds himself or herself in a new and deeper relationship with the Lord, with a new awareness of the Lord's love and presence. He or she discovers new power in Christian ministry, in teaching or in speaking about the Lord, in helping others, and in serving the Lord in other ways. There comes a new and much stronger appreciation of the Bible and new enthusiasm for reading it reverently and prayerfully as God's word now.

Very often, even outside pentecostal and charismatic groups, baptism in the Spirit results in the gift of praying in tongues. It sometimes results in other new gifts: praying for healing, powerful intercessory prayer, spiritual power in combating the forces of evil, prophecy, spiritual leadership, and other gifts of ministry. And, always, along with a new outpouring of his Spirit and of his gifts, the Lord strengthens, reinforces, the gifts the person needs for his state in life. I found myself much stronger in my ministry as a priest, more prayerful at Mass, and greatly reinforced in the gifts of my religious order: celibacy for the Lord, discernment of spirits, prayerfulness in my work, and others. The Lord gives us what we need, and much more.

Often people feel elated and enthusiastic for the things of the Spirit for some time after they receive this new outpouring. The time of spiritual consolation and gladness and joy in the Lord can last several days, or some months, or even a year or more. What happens then?

After the baptism in the Spirit.
Because one of the effects of the baptism in the Holy Spirit is a new and felt relationship with the Lord, prayer becomes easier, more satisfying, more consoling. The time for personal prayer passes quickly. The person newly baptized in the Spirit finds it easy to pray. Often people enter into real contemplative prayer with the baptism in the Spirit, especially people who have already had a serious prayer life for several years.

But then, after a while, the enthusiasm passes, the good feelings fade, prayer can become drier and less satisfying and less consoling. This quite normal and common experience can discourage people. They can feel that they are somehow losing all the fruits of the baptism in the Spirit, that they are drifting away from the Lord, that they are losing the Lord in some way that they do not understand. They sometimes do not know why, and they do not know what to do.

Why, after a time of glad enthusiasm, does the Lord lead us into the desert, where we feel his absence even though we know he is present, where we find prayer and the practice of Christian virtue more difficult? When I was baptized in the Spirit, the lights went on. Now they dim and seem to go out. Why?

Because the Lord calls me to greater Christian maturity. He wants to purify me.

He wants to purify me of what? Of whatever attachments would keep me from a closer union with him. He wants to purify me of whatever might present an obstacle in me to greater intimacy with him. Not only sin, but also any attachment to his gifts that could make me value the gifts more than the giver. So the Lord wants to purify me of any attachment to my feeling good and enthusiastic and close to him—at least to the extent that those attachments can get in the way of my closer walk with him.

He purifies me by taking away, usually gradually, the feelings of joy, of enthusiasm, of *elan*—those feelings that keep me warm, that can lead me to think I am a lot holier than I am. He wants me to love him for himself and because he saves me, not because he gives me good feelings and glad moods and eagerness for the things of God. A bird tied to a tree cannot fly. If he is tied with a chain, he cannot fly; if he is tied with a thread, he still cannot fly. The Lord wants not only to free me from the chains of sin but also to untie the threads of attachment to my feeling good. He wants to purify me.

This purification is a call to greater Christian maturity. It can be a sobering experience. It should not discourage me or make me falter in seeking a closer union with the Lord.

The lights are out. I can receive the Lord's love in the dark. It is the Lord I really want, and I want him much more than I want to feel his presence or to feel good about him. I can, in my quiet time with the Lord, remain quietly in the dark with him, not feeling but knowing in faith that he is here, he loves me, he holds me.

The darkness may last a long time. I want to hold fast to the Lord in the dark. I want to walk in the desert dryness with the Lord, faithfully. Above all, I want to be more faithful than ever to him in prayer.

Personal Prayer

The heart and center of Christianity is personal relationship with Jesus Christ risen. I want that relationship, then, to hold first place in my life, to act as the central relationship in my life—organizing my other relationships, synthesizing them, giving them meaning and new life.

The heart and center of a living interpersonal relationship with Jesus Christ is prayer—in particular, personal prayer. I do not mean that group prayer, family prayer, church services, and the Mass have little or no importance. On the contrary. But prayer with others can always to some degree fall into formalism or acting, because I need the support of others. Prayer with others needs personal prayer—prayer alone, by myself, to nourish my relationship with the Lord so that my prayer with others will be authentic, honest, real prayer.

Furthermore, my personal prayer will keep my relationship with the Lord alive and strong. What do I need in order to have a life of personal prayer? What conditions must I meet, make, in my daily life so as to have a healthy prayer life in which the Lord can unite me more closely to himself? I need: daily fidelity, simplicity, and trust. Let us take these one at a time.

Fidelity.
Relationship with the Lord, like any interpersonal relationship, calls for discipline and to a great extent depends on discipline. If I want a good and loving relationship with someone, I need to spend time with that person. If I hold someone important in my life, I give him or her time. I want to be faithful to the Lord, to his love for me. My faithfulness to him in prayer forms a part of my response to his love. This means that I need to have a fixed amount of time every day that I dedicate to prayer, that I give exclusively to the Lord.

How much time? That depends. Perhaps an hour, perhaps twenty minutes. Of course, I want to pray all during the day, to live as much as I can with my eyes fixed on the Lord. But I need a time of fixed length when I can be completely alone with the Lord, quiet, for him only, with nothing else to do, with no outside distractions. It might be before others in the house awake in the morning, or after they go to bed, or during my lunch hour, or at any time when I can find a quiet place and be with the Lord. Or I might pray twice daily—for example, twenty minutes in the morning and twenty minutes in the evening.

In any case, I need to be faithful every day to the amount of time that I have determined to give to the Lord. Not that the Lord is a timekeeper; he does not judge me because I miss my prayer time with him one or two days. I need to be faithful because my fidelity to my quiet time with the Lord expresses the degree of my commitment to him, the degree of my response to his love.

If the Lord has an important place in my life, in my heart, then I will find time to pray, to be with him, no matter how busy my day. If something comes up and I cannot pray at my regularly fixed time, I can make it up later in the day. My fidelity to my regular amount of prayer time measures my response to the Lord's love for me.

Simplicity.

True prayer is simple, childlike, uncluttered by a lot of thoughts and ideas. Real prayer speaks straight from the heart. It says simply, "I love you, Lord," and, "Thank you for loving me." The best prayer is the simplest prayer: union of hearts, the union of my heart with the Lord's heart. Simple prayer says little or nothing. It looks with love at the Lord. It speaks his name with trust and with love; and it accepts his love, resting in it and trusting in it.

To anyone who wants to pray, the Lord says, "Learn from me, for I am lowly and humble of heart; and you will find rest for your souls" (Mt 11:29). I can learn from him to be lowly, small, humble before him. He tells me to make myself small, to humble myself like a little child before him (see Mt 18:4).

When Martha complained that she had to prepare and serve the meal herself, asking Jesus to get her sister Mary to help her, Jesus answered her, "Martha, Martha, you worry and fret about so many things; and yet few are needed, indeed only one. It is Mary who has chosen the better part; it is not to be taken from her" (Lk 10:41-42). Mary sat quietly at Jesus' feet, looking at him with love and listening to him—not only with her ears but with her heart. I can be "busy about many things" in my prayer—doing, thinking, talking. The Lord tells me that the "better part" is to be quiet, not busy, and to sit at his feet with reverent love. And he will teach me himself.

Prayer is like dancing. When I (Robert Faricy) was twelve years old, my parents sent me to dancing school to learn ballroom dancing, hoping that the experience would help to make me a civilized person. The dancing teacher would put a record on the record player—a waltz, for example—and each of us would choose a partner to dance with. I was the smallest in the class; all the girls were bigger than I was—a lot bigger. Whatever girl I had as a partner would drag me around the dance floor in spite of my protests that the man should lead. The girls too, after all, were just learning to dance.

Prayer is like dancing. Whether you are a man or a woman, the Lord has the man's part in the dance. He leads; I follow. And if he dances slowly, I do not want to go fast. I want to follow his lead.

I make a mistake when I try to over-program my prayer. Prayer is simple: I go to the Lord simply, I look at him with love, and then I follow his lead.

Trust.

To pray, I need to trust the Lord. I need to trust his love for me. I need to hang on to the fact that Jesus loves me personally. Not just as one among many, a face in the crowd; I need to know that he calls me by name.

And he does. Jesus died for me on the cross as though I were the only other person who ever walked on earth. When he comes to me now, in my daily life and in a special way in my prayer, he comes personally, saying my name. He loves me, and because he is God, his love is infinitely powerful. It empowers me to pray, to come to him in prayer and to receive his love.

Pray with me now:

Lord Jesus, teach me to pray.
Give me the gift of trusting in you more.
Help me to pray simply, like a little child,
without many ideas and words.
Help me to stay faithful to my time with you every
day. Amen.

Ways to Pray

What should I do when I pray? How do I spend my quiet time with the Lord? What do I do?

What method of prayer should I use? Should I use a method at all?

Here in this section we suggest some simple ways to pray, probably not structured enough to be called methods. You might use any of them or all of them, even combining them, or pray some other way. The rule is: Use what helps you.

I want to pray the way the Lord leads me to pray. How do I know how he is leading me to pray? He leads me in the way that helps me the most to relate to him, the way that gives me the greatest facility in remaining close to him. Whatever way, at the moment, makes it easiest for me to be most united with the Lord—that is the way he is leading me, and so that is how I want to pray. Different ways for different people, and different ways for the same person at different times.

My criterion, then, in deciding what to do in prayer is this: whatever helps me the most to relate to the Lord.

PRAY

For example, if I go regularly to prayer meetings, I might follow a general prayer meeting format. Most charismatic prayer meetings begin with praise and continue with more praise interspersed with Bible readings, prophecies, and inspired prayers or statements. There frequently follows a teaching, then prayer of petition and thanksgiving for favors received from the Lord. The meeting usually closes with a hymn or a prayer.

I can, in my personal prayer, have my own prayer meeting with the Lord. I can follow the acronym PRAY—*P* for praise, *R* for rest in the Lord, *A* for ask, *Y* for yes to the Lord.

P. My prayer can begin with praise. I might begin by singing a favorite hymn to the Lord. For personal prayer, hymns that are already prayers serve the best—for example, "Just a Closer Walk with Thee," or "Holy God, We Praise Thy Name," or some other hymn or song addressed directly to God, praising or thanking or adoring God. Then, if I have the gift of tongues, I could continue to praise the Lord in tongues, singing or praying quietly in tongues. If it seems right, I can continue to alternate hymns, quiet praise and adoration, and perhaps praise in tongues.

R. The Lord might give me a reading from the Bible. If I feel he wants to show me a passage, I can open the Bible and see what he has for me. I can read the passage slowly, letting it sink in, resting in it prayerfully. Or, on some occasions, the Lord could even give me a personal prophecy as food for my prayer.

So I have already begun the second and principal part of my prayer: resting in the Lord. This is a quiet time with the Lord. I rest in him and let him teach me and love me and form and transform me in his own secret way. I might use a Bible text to help me to enter into relationship with him—one he gives me and that I find by prayerfully opening the Bible, or the Gospel of the Mass of the day, or the next few lines of one of the Gospels that I am working through day by day in my prayer. I might use centering prayer. However I pray, I want to rest in the Lord in some way, letting him love me and responding to his love.

A. Toward the end of my prayer time, I can present to the Lord my prayers of petition. I tell him simply for whom I want to pray, naming the persons, placing them in his hands. I lift up to the Lord my own requests; I pray for what I need. And I thank him for all he has done for me in response to previous requests.

Υ. I can conclude my prayer by saying yes to the Lord. I might sing the great "Amen" to one of the melodies used at Mass after the Eucharistic Prayer. *Amen* means "so be it" or "yes, Lord, to what you want." Or I might sing a favorite hymn, perhaps a hymn in which I can somehow say yes to the Lord's love and to whatever he wants. Or I can simply thank him for my prayer and say yes to his love and to his will.

Centering prayer.

Another way to pray is to use centering prayer. I can take one word—the name of Jesus, for example—and put it in my heart. I speak the word *Jesus* silently in my heart, repeating it very slowly. Rather than say *Jesus,* I let the word—as it were—speak itself over and over in my heart. In this way, I use the word *Jesus* to center myself on the Lord Jesus. I center myself on his name, repeating it silently and slowly in my heart. And, by centering myself on his name, I center myself on him; I let him draw me into union with him.

Centering prayer does not depend at all on thoughts or ideas. It is a contemplative kind of prayer, a silent nonconceptual prayer. The only content of centering prayer is the one word. When that word is *Jesus,* then the prayer content is Jesus himself and my union of love with him.

Centering prayer helps me to center myself on the Lord, to enter more deeply into loving union with him, and to avoid distractions. I can use centering prayer during the entire time of my prayer period. Or I can use it during the "resting in the Lord" phase of a private prayer meeting (PRAY) with the Lord. Or I can combine it with using the Bible for prayer.

Using the Gospels for prayer.
The whole Bible is the inspired word of God, and any part of the Bible can be used for prayer. The four Gospels, however, have a special importance as paths to closer union with the Lord in prayer.

I can take a brief action of a Gospel, a few verses that tell about a healing, a small part of a teaching by Jesus, or any small portion of a Gospel, and use it for my prayer. For example, I might read the passage slowly and prayerfully, then enter into relationship with the Lord on the basis of what I have before me in the Gospel. I can talk to the Lord simply, in my own words. I can just rest there, looking at him with love, letting the Gospel words sink in. Or I can use centering prayer, repeating the name of Jesus slowly in my heart. Or I can use a version of centering prayer based on the portion of the Gospel that I have just read. If I have read the passage about the healing of the blind man Bartimaeus, I can repeat over and over his words, "Lord, that I may see." If I have before me the words of Jesus, "Learn from me, for I am meek and humble of heart," I can pray silently, repeating the words over and over in my heart, "Teach me, Jesus."

Other ways to pray.
There are many other ways to pray. The best ways are the simplest ones.

But sometimes I find myself too distracted to pray. I have matters on my mind that crowd in on my prayer, that fill my heart, that distract me from giving myself totally to the Lord in prayer. More about this in the next section.

Jesus Is Lord of My Prayer and Lord of My Life

The phrase "Jesus is Lord" is one of the most ancient in Christian tradition. It occurs six times in the Pauline writings of the New Testament. For example, in Philippians 2:9-11:

> God has highly exalted him and bestowed on him the name which is above every name, that at the name of Jesus every knee should bow . . . and every tongue confess that Jesus Christ is Lord, to the glory of God the Father.

In this text, the "name which is above every name" is not the name Jesus but the title Lord. Jesus has the highest title, a title that in fact belongs properly to God and that the Old Testament gives only to God.

Jesus is Lord not only because he has a title. His lordship is real. We know from the first three chapters of the Letter to the Ephesians that "he [the Father] has put all things under his [Jesus'] feet and made him, as the ruler of everything, the head of the Church, which is his body, the fullness of him who fills the whole creation" (1:22). Jesus is Lord in the sense that he *fills* the whole world, is present everywhere in it and all through it by the influence of his risen and universal love. And he is Lord in the sense that he *rules* everything in the world; he has the sovereignty over all creation.

The Letter to the Colossians understands the world as holding together in the Lord Jesus, as being somehow suspended from him, as depending on him for its very existence. "In him all things hold together" (1:17). Jesus is Lord because he brings everything together in himself "to reconcile to himself all things" (1:20). The Letter to the Hebrews goes even further; Jesus is Lord and high priest who intercedes for us at the right hand of the Father (1:10; 2:8; 6:20-8:13).

Jesus: Lord of my life.

This Lord of all creation, ruler and sustainer and filler of everything, is also my own personal Lord, the Lord of my life, who calls me by my name to live in close interpersonal relationship with him. He fills all creation with his love, and he fills me with his love. He rules the world, and he wants to direct my life to a greater fullness in him. Like the world does, I depend on him even for my existence. Jesus gives meaning to the world and to its history; and he gives meaning to me and to my life. He intercedes for the world at the right hand of the Father; and he prays for me, lifting me up to the Father.

Jesus is my Lord as well as Lord of the universe. The Father's plan for the world is to unite all things in Jesus, under the lordship of Jesus (Eph 1:10). That is, the Father wants to reconcile everything in Jesus Christ, all things whether on earth or in heaven. This is God's plan for the world. And it is God's plan for me: that I be more and more united interiorly; that everything in me be reconciled, unified, integrated, in Jesus Christ; and that, in Jesus, I be more and more reconciled with the Father in the Holy Spirit.

Jesus wants to give me unity of person in him, to integrate all the parts of myself into a unified whole in him, to knit up all the frazzled segments of myself into a new unity under his lordship. This is his project for me. He does this work mainly in and through my personal prayer. And it is in my quiet time with him that I cooperate with his project for me.

Jesus: Lord of my prayer.

Jesus invites me to place all my concerns, worries, problems, firmly in his hands when I pray. Whatever might or does distract me in prayer I can lift up to the Lord, putting the matter in his hands.

In fact, I can put everything in my life into the Lord's hands when I pray: my fears, anxieties, failures; my plans, hopes, successes; my choices, decisions, options. Jesus is interested in everything in my life. He is—and he wants to be even more—Lord of my life. I cooperate with his project of pulling me together and centering me on him when I bring whatever is on my mind to him in prayer.

When I put anything in the Lord's hands in prayer, under his lordship, into his loving care, then that thing becomes more integrated into my personal relationship with him. The more I do this, the more my life—through my prayer—will become unified, integrated, centered on Jesus.

For example, if I worry about a money problem, I can, in my personal prayer, give that problem to the

Lord, putting it in his hands and trusting in him for the future. I do not simply put the problem out of my mind. I put it, as it were, into his; and then I can stop worrying about it—or at least worry less, according to the faith that he gives me.

Again, if a personal relationship has become a serious concern—if, for instance, I cannot get along with someone at work that I do need to get along with—I can pray for that person, placing him or her in Jesus' hands, putting the whole relationship under his lordship, trusting in him to straighten out the relationship.

Distractions.

The distractions that I have in my prayer can help me. They indicate to me the parts of my life that are not yet completely integrated into my relationship with the Lord.

For example, if someone I love comes up in my prayer as a distraction, that means that my relationship with that person has not yet been fully integrated into my relationship with Jesus. Rather than simply dismissing the distraction, I can prayerfully place my relationship with that person into Jesus' hands, under his lordship.

The reason that the person is a distraction is this: Something in my relationship with that person is not fully under Jesus' lordship, not completely integrated into my relationship with Jesus. If it were, then the person would not be a distraction; he or she would be, from the beginning, a subject of prayer. That is, because something in my relationship to the person I love leads me away from Jesus in my life, therefore it leads me away from Jesus in my prayer. Because something in my relationship to this person is not fully oriented to the Lord, the person becomes a distraction in my prayer.

What is this something in the relationship that leads me away from the Lord in my life and in my prayer? Possessiveness. I might think that I love the person too much, but this is never the case. We never love people too much; we should always love them more. The problem is that I tend to love possessively, treating the other person more as an object than a subject. I perhaps use the other person to gratify my own needs. I tend to possess the person I love rather than leaving him or her free.

The Lord wants to teach me to love the way he loves me, with an open hand, leaving the other person free. He wants to teach me to love the other person unselfishly, to love not less but more.

When, in prayer, I pray for the person I love, lifting that person up to the Lord and bringing our relationship explicitly under the lordship of Jesus, then I cooperate with Jesus' project to integrate my life, to integrate this relationship of love into my personal relationship with him. I cooperate with the Lord's work in my life by bringing the person and my love for him or her to the Lord. I can and ought to do this as often as the person becomes a distraction. Eventually the person will no longer be a distraction but a subject of intercessory prayer. Whenever I think of him or her, I will be led immediately to the Lord to pray for the person.

The same procedure is useful for any distraction: I turn the content of the distraction into prayer; I pray for whom or what distracts me. Let us say that someone has hurt me or hurt my feelings, or both. Upset, I find it difficult to pray. The hurt is on my mind, an obstacle to my relating easily to the Lord, a distraction. I can turn the distraction into a prayer, into a way of relating to the Lord.

I forgive the person in my heart. I pray for the person, lifting him or her up to Jesus. And I ask the Lord to heal the hurt, to console me. I might offer my suffering to the Father in union with Jesus' suffering for me on the cross. I might ask for the gifts of compassion and understanding toward this person who has hurt me.

The Lord will answer my prayer. He will gradually heal the hurts in my heart. He will use what has happened to draw me closer to himself.

Besides positive relationships of love or admiration and negative relationships of hurt or resentment or anger, other matters can show up as distractions in prayer. I can use them in the same way.

If my work distracts me, I offer it up to the Lord, putting it under his lordship. If a talk I have to give or something I have to say in the future distracts me, then, rather than plan what I will say, I give it to the

Lord, ask his help and his guidance, let him inspire me as to what I will say. He can inspire me right at the moment in my prayer, or later in his own time.

If family problems or future plans or possible or real failures or setbacks distract me, I turn them over to the Lord. I want him to be Lord over my whole life and over everything in it.

Freedom and contemplation.

By cooperating with Jesus' project for me—to center my life on him—I grow in freedom. I gradually become freer from whatever might lead me away from the Lord: sin, fear, discouragement, anxiety, unrealistic guilt feelings, and all the other negative bonds that hold me back from closer union with the Lord.

When I look at Jesus with love in my prayer, putting everything trustingly into his hands, he leads me to greater freedom—freedom to love him and to love others in a mature way without possessiveness, freedom to respond to his love and to the love that other persons have for me. He helps me to grow in holiness.

Holiness is the infinite capacity to love and to receive love. That is why only God is truly holy: only God can love and receive love infinitely.

But I can grow in holiness. The principal way to grow in holiness is to keep my eyes lovingly on Jesus, to look at Jesus with love. We call this "contemplation."

TWO

Contemplating Jesus

TO *CONTEMPLATE* MEANS "TO LOOK AT STEADILY." Christian contemplation is looking at Jesus with love. It is sitting at Jesus' feet, looking at him, listening to him, receiving love and strength from him.

The prayer of just looking at Jesus with love will lead me to know him. I can know a lot about some famous singer, or football star, but to know about a person is different from knowing the person. Through being with Jesus in prayer, I can come to know him better. Of course, I want to know more about a person who loves me and whom I love. But beyond that, I want to know the person better. Jesus knows me entirely, accepts me totally, loves me intensely, and calls me by name. And he leads me to love him and to know him better through love—through his love of me and my loving response.

This knowledge of Jesus—which comes from sitting at his feet, looking at him, listening to him—may seem obscure, vague, but it is really a growing experience of Jesus, so that one day I am surprised to find I really *do* know Jesus and do really love him.

Feelings do count. Sometimes, of course, I must pray in dryness, darkness, without any special feelings, perhaps even feeling out of touch with the Lord. But ordinarily, my contemplating Jesus will involve my feelings.

It will depend too on the kind of person I am. I can only relate to Jesus as myself. I do not have to try to be someone else, or different from myself, when I come to Jesus in prayer. The way I love him and know him will be just the way it is between us: Jesus—who made me, knows and loves me—chose me, as I am.

Christian contemplation is knowledge through love. Through his Holy Spirit, Jesus pours his love into my heart. That love, his for me, empowers me to love him back. *Contemplation* means knowing Jesus through the love he has for me and through the love I have for him.

So Paul in the Letter to the Ephesians encourages us to be "rooted and grounded in love" so that we may "have power to comprehend with all the saints, what is the breadth and length and height and depth and to know the love of Christ which surpasses knowledge, that [we] may be filled with all the fullness of God" (3:17-19).

Jesus Remembers

There are some people who would like to pray more than they do but hold back because they "don't know what to say." But it is not necessary to say anything in prayer. One can just look at Jesus, in love, as he is now. Of course, we do not see him, or even need to imagine what he looks like, nor do we need to feel love. I *know* that Jesus is alive, I *know* he is always looking at me with love, though I may be the blackest of sinners. So I can just kneel or sit in his presence, and that is prayer.

Looking at Jesus in a gospel passage.
Another way to pray is to look at Jesus in the mysteries of his life, to look at these mysteries with him, as he sees them now. St. Ignatius of Loyola gives a simple method. He says: first, read a gospel passage; second, look briefly at the scene—see Jesus and the others there, speaking, acting; third, ask for the grace you want, which is to know Jesus better, to love him more, and to follow him more closely. These three points take only a few minutes.

But then what? I can talk to Jesus about the scene—Jesus now alive, in heaven, in me, or here in this room or church. I can ask him questions about the event, about the things he said and did. This will lead me to acts of love, compassion, trust, sorrow for sin, or praise and admiration. The key to this kind of prayer is not that I remember what Jesus said or did but that Jesus *remembers*. Jesus remembers, and he is present, risen, here with me in my prayer, to take me into his memory, into his heart. I can rest there, letting him quietly and gently draw me into the essence of his memory of what he did, of what he said, of what he underwent. If I feel nothing, if nothing seems to be going on, it does not matter. Prayer is the Lord's work more than it is mine, and what goes on is always deeper in me than I can reach.

If when I go to pray I am always "busy" about it, always "saying prayers" or sticking rigidly to a method I was once taught, I may be missing a grace the Lord is offering, the grace of a prayer that goes beyond words. God leads in prayer; it is his activity more than it is mine. If I insist on doing it my way, I could find myself alone in a desert of dryness and dissatisfaction.

A slow repeating of the holy name Jesus as I look at him in glory, or look with him at the mysteries of his life and death, is another way of contemplative prayer. People whose only prayer seems to be the rosary often pray in a contemplative way, not with "busy" thoughts but with an interior tasting of the mysteries, which leads to knowledge and love of Jesus.

Two notes:
First, it is well to begin by coming into the Lord's presence, or rather by adverting to his presence, for we are at every moment present before the beatific vision of God—present blindly, and often too "busy about many things" to remember. We turn to the presence of God. Some people find that praying for a few moments in tongues brings them face-to-face

with God. Then we do whatever the Lord indicates. We can just stay there, not thinking about what he is like but just that he *is*—reaching out to him without words, or resting in his presence, or leaning against the heart of Jesus. Our love does not matter here, we just let Jesus love us in the way he wants, this moment.

Second, the time and place of prayer are important. St. John of the Cross says, "Do not make light of the trysting place." If I have a time and place where I regularly wait upon the Lord, he will honor it. I go there not to seek prayer but to seek Jesus and the Father whom he reveals.

An example of the prayer of looking at Jesus in a gospel message.

To contemplate Jesus in some event of his life, something he says or does or something that happened to him, I can choose a gospel passage. I might choose a few verses from Jesus' words at the last supper from St. John's Gospel (chapters 13 through 17), or a healing miracle, or Jesus walking on the water. Or I can use the gospel for the Mass of the day (many people do this). Or the Sunday gospel could be used for that week, repeating the same gospel passage every day.

As an example, let us take the gospel for the feast of the Epiphany (Mt 2:1-12). We will take things step by step.

1. First, I need a time every day, perhaps early in

the morning, or just before I go to bed at night. It could be after Mass, or on my way home from work or school. And a place: my room, or a corner of the house where we have a shrine, or in church, or somewhere else where I can be alone and quiet with the Lord.

2. I recall that Jesus is here. Maybe I praise him for a moment in tongues. I offer him my prayer.

3. I read Matthew 2:1-12.

4. I briefly imagine the event, seeing the wise men, perhaps recalling some picture I have seen.

5. I ask in my own words for the grace I want: "Lord Jesus, teach me to *know you better*, so that I can love you more and follow you more closely."

6. I settle quietly into my prayer, letting the Lord lead me, returning to him from any distractions I might have, centering on him. Perhaps I repeat his name slowly in my heart, "Jesus, Jesus, Jesus." I spend the full time I have decided on for my prayer—ten minutes or twenty, a half hour, an hour.

7. When I am finished I thank Jesus.

Prayer:
Lord Jesus, teach me to pray.
Teach me to look at you
and to "taste and see that the Lord is good."
I put myself entirely into your hands.
I give you myself.
I do not know how to pray;
I am helpless.

Guide me.
Amen.
Mary, you are my mother.
Get for me from Jesus the graces I need to pray.
Watch over me, and help me along in my prayer.
Amen.

Contemplating Jesus in the Mass

The greatest contemplative prayer is the sacrifice of the Mass. The action is Jesus'. My part is contemplative: awareness, receptivity. I need to be alive to what is going on, my eyes on Jesus.

All the power of God is here in the Mass. Sometimes we experience God's power, but always we believe in it.

During the Scripture readings of the Mass, Jesus is present in the power of his word, speaking to me in the mighty power of his word. If I listen, with my heart open to receive, to contemplate, then the power of the word will enter my life. St. John's first letter summarizes the essence of contemplating the word: "Something which has existed since the beginning; that we have heard, and we have seen with our own eyes; that we have watched, and touched with our hands; the Word, who is life" (1 Jn 1:1).

The word listened to with an open heart will change me by its power. It will convict me and animate me: "Is not my word like fire, says the Lord, and like a hammer which breaks the rock in pieces?" (Jer 23:29). "The word of God is living and active" (Heb 4:12). It will cleanse me; Jesus says, "You are ... clean by the word which I have spoken to you" (Jn 15:3). The word heals me: "He sent forth his word, and healed them" (Ps 107:20). "No herb, no poultice cured them, but it was your word, Lord, which heals all things" (Wis 16:12).

The power of God is as often gentle as mighty; it fills me with sweetness. We have "tasted the good word of God" (Heb 6:5). "How sweet are thy words to my taste, sweeter than honey to my mouth" (Ps 119:103). Sitting at Jesus' feet, listening to his word in the Scripture readings at Mass, I receive the power of his word as he promised: "The word that goes from my mouth does not return to me empty, without carrying out my will and succeeding in what it was sent to do" (Is 55:11).

As the Mass continues, we move into the power of the cross and blood of Jesus. Jesus offers himself to his Father, in the Holy Spirit, their mutual love and their love which embraces us. As Jesus is lifted up in the consecration, his promise becomes effective: "When I am lifted up from the earth, I shall draw all men to myself" (Jn 12:32). The rebellious Israelites were bitten by serpents in the desert. God instructed Moses to make a bronze serpent and lift it up on a pole. When the sick and sinful Israelites came out of their tents and looked up at the bronze figure, power went out from it and touched them for healing and forgiveness (Nm 21:9). Jesus said, "The Son of Man must be lifted up as Moses lifted up the serpent in the desert, so that everyone who believes may have eternal life in him" (Jn 3:13-15). The consecration is this moment in faith for us. As we "look on the one whom we have pierced" (see Jn 19:37), power goes out from him.

At the foot of the cross we can pray, "May his blood be upon us and upon our children" (see Mt 27:26)—not now for condemnation, but the blood of the new covenant, which, offered in the Mass and received in Holy Communion, ransoms, forgives, purifies, frees, and preserves me for everlasting life. The power of the precious blood is "the ransom that was paid to free you from a useless way of life . . . [paid] in the precious blood of . . . Christ" (1 Pt 1:18-19). "Through his blood, we gain our freedom, the forgiveness of our sins" (Eph 1:7). "The blood of Jesus . . . purifies us from all sin" (1 Jn 1:7).

As we continue to contemplate Jesus in the Mass, we come into the power of the presence of God. At the little elevation the church teaches us that contemplation—and all Christian prayer—is trinitarian, that my prayer, my life, is nothing less than the prayer and life of Jesus in the Trinity. We look up at the elevated body and blood of Jesus, risen and glorious, and pray:

Through him [Jesus],
with him,

in him,
in the unity of the Holy Spirit,
all glory and honor is yours,
almighty Father.

It is through Jesus that "we . . . have access in one Spirit to the Father" (Eph 2:18). And "all the promises of God find their yes in him. That is why we utter the Amen through him to the glory of God" (2 Cor 1:20).

The presence of God is most powerful in me after Holy Communion. Though I can never grasp the reality, I know that in that time "we, with our unveiled faces reflecting like mirrors the brightness of the Lord, all grow brighter and brighter as we are turned into the image that we reflect; this is the work of the Lord who is Spirit" (2 Cor 3:18). This is the union to which contemplative prayer leads. I surrender to Jesus' action, his love; I let him minister to me.

The Gift of Tongues

Why is it that so many men and women have found that the baptism in the Spirit has given them a whole new relationship with the Lord? Why have so many found that the baptism in the Spirit and the gift of tongues have led them for the first time to real contemplative prayer, or to a new and deeper contemplation? It seems clear that the great grace of the charismatic renewal, whether in a group or alone, is a renewed interpersonal relationship with Jesus Christ in personal prayer, a breakthrough in contemplative prayer. Why?

For one thing, of course, the baptism in the Spirit is a great grace and is followed by an outpouring of graces and gifts. For another, many people receive the gift of tongues when the Lord baptizes them in the Spirit, or perhaps at some time later, and the gift of tongues is itself a gift of contemplative prayer. To receive the gift of tongues *is* to receive a gift of contemplative prayer.

When I pray in silent contemplation, I simply remain without words, or with only a few words, in the Lord's presence, looking at him in faith. I do not have any great things to say, any particular thoughts or ideas. I am just looking lovingly at the Lord looking at me. I am silently contemplating him.

I do something similar when I pray in tongues. I do not have any specific thoughts or ideas. I do not understand what I am saying or singing in tongues. When I sing in tongues, I do not speak or sing a language, at least not in the vast majority of cases. Scientific analysis of tapes of tongues-speaking has never found the structure of a real language. The meaning is not in the sounds, as though they were words that represented ideas. The meaning of prayer in tongues lies in the heart.

When I pray in tongues, I simply look at the Lord in faith and sing to him some syllables that do not have any special meaning, as an infant babbles to his or her mother. The infant communicates something in general, but not any particular ideas. And the mother understands, is pleased, and responds. Praying in tongues, I am like a baby, looking at the Lord with love, praising, or asking or being thankful—in general, expressing what is beyond language.

Prayer in tongues is vocal contemplation. Singing in tongues is sung contemplation. I can contemplate the Lord silently or out loud.

When I (Sister Lucy) came to write my contribution to this chapter, I sat down before the Lord to ask him what I should write and to pray for all those who would read it. I found myself praying in tongues, then remaining still and continuing to look at Jesus in faith. Someone has written: "Why do Catholic charismatics pray in tongues? The answer is, because they don't know the words!" That is exactly it. St. Paul says: "We do not know how to pray as we ought, but the Spirit himself prays for us with sighs too deep for words. And he who searches the heart knows what is the mind of the Spirit" (Rom 8:26-27). When I do not know what to say or what to ask, when a situation is beyond me, and especially when I realize a little of the holiness of God, I cannot find adequate words, so I pray in tongues, asking the Holy Spirit within me to take over the meaning of my prayer.

Sometimes tongues come spontaneously, and I sing in love and admiration. Sometimes I begin deliberately to pray in tongues. Certainly tongues are always under our control, even when spontaneous. It is an extra gift from the Lord for prayer.

In my experience of spiritual direction, I (Robert Faricy) have found the gift of tongues to be the single biggest help toward contemplative prayer. This is because to receive the gift of tongues is to receive a gift of contemplative prayer. So, of course, when a person receives a gift of vocal contemplation—praying in tongues—that person usually finds silent contemplation easier and more attractive.

There is an analogy between praying in tongues and saying the rosary in such a way as to contemplate the mysteries of the life of Jesus while saying the words of the Hail Mary. When I say the rosary, I "meditate" on the various mysteries; that is, I look at—contemplate—Jesus or his mother in the different mysteries. I say the words, but my attention is more on the Lord, at whom I am looking. Praying in tongues is similar; I pay no attention to the syllables I am saying, because I am looking at the Lord, contemplating him.

Many people who have this gift begin their daily personal prayer with a brief period—perhaps thirty seconds or a few minutes—of praying in tongues. In that way they enter into the Lord's presence and remain there silently in contemplative prayer. The principal use of the gift of tongues is not, as many may suppose, in prayer groups or in charismatic conferences. It is in personal prayer: "One who speaks in a tongue speaks not to men but to God; for no one understands him, but he utters mysteries in the Spirit" (1 Cor 14:2).

How can I receive the gift of tongues? St. Paul says, "I want you all to speak in tongues" (1 Cor 14:5). If the gift is not only for the prayer group nor only for those baptized in the Holy Spirit, and if it will help me in my prayer and lead me to the Lord, then I want it. How can I get it? Not by any technique. But how then can I receive the gift of tongues?

By asking the Giver.

Invite one or a few people who have the gift of tongues to pray over you, in tongues, for that gift. Then, looking at the Lord in faith, speak or sing some sounds to the Lord. Then let it flow.

Or go somewhere where you can be alone, kneel down, and ask the Lord to give you the gift of praying in tongues. Then, with faith in him and in his goodness, look at him with eyes of faith. Open your mouth. And begin to sing or say syllables to him, like a baby who has not yet learned to talk. If you are praying, this is the gift of tongues. The discomfort you feel is your pride hurting; you will get over that.

Then thank the Lord for the new gift of prayer he has given you.

Contemplating Jesus with His Mother

"Sir, we should like to see Jesus" (Jn 12:22)—so the Greeks approached Philip. The most effective intermediary in our seeking to "see Jesus" is his mother. The divine economy was that the Son of God came to the world through Mary. She is the efficacious way for us to go to him. Of course, the best prayer is always directly to Jesus, to our Father, to the Holy Spirit. Nonetheless, Mary is a chosen mediatrix, because the Lord is always to be found where Mary is.

Almost the first words about her in the Gospels are, "Rejoice, highly favored one; the Lord is with you." If we spend time with Mary, the mother whom Jesus bequeathed to us in his dying moment, we can pray to God with her, we can contemplate the Holy Trinity with her, we can receive her Son from her.

It was in wordless contemplation that Mary received the Word incarnate. "When all things were in quiet silence and the night had but half run its course, thy almighty Word leaped down from the heaven, from thy royal throne" (Wis 18:14-15). The Word entered the womb of Mary, and she communed with him, loved him, during nine months as she went about her active life—traveling, helping Elizabeth, journeying again to Bethlehem.

When he was born, the shepherds "found Mary and Joseph, and the baby lying in the manger" (Lk 2:16). Similarly, when he was manifested to all the nations in the person of the magi, "they saw the child with his mother Mary" (Mt 2:11). Mary never draws attention to herself, but always leads our eyes to Jesus. At Cana she directed the waiters to Jesus: "Do whatever he tells you" (Jn 2:5).

"My spirit exults in God my Savior, because *he has looked upon* his lowly handmaid" (Lk 1:46). "Jesus *looked steadily at* him [the rich young man] and loved him" (Mk 10:21). This is the other side of the coin of contemplative prayer: prayer is not so much that I look at Jesus but that he looks on his lowly servant, that he looks steadily at me and loves me.

Our Lady can teach me to appreciate and take seriously this personal love that Jesus has for me. God's love for me is not just benevolence. Benevolence did not lead the Father to give his only Son for me (see Jn 3:16). Benevolence did not lead Jesus to the cross. The love that Jesus feels for me is, like all deep love, strong, tender, in earnest, and demanding.

> Love is strong as Death,
> jealously relentless as Sheol.
> The flash of it is a flash of fire,
> a flame of Yahweh himself.
> Love no flood can quench,
> no torrents drown. (Sg 8:6, JB)

"Love no flood can quench" was poured from the

heart of Jesus into the heart of Mary. It kept her faithful even to the cross of Jesus.

We can pray:

> My heavenly mother, how dull and dense I often am, how slow to believe in the wonder, the truth, of Jesus' love for me. Intercede for me, teach me yourself. I am your small child; teach me, guide me to Jesus, now and at the hour of my death.

Love and Discernment

All of us who have received a new life in baptism and have that new life released more and more in us by the outpouring of the Holy Spirit want to "walk in newness of life," want to "live by the Spirit" (Gal 5:25). So we depend for every step on the direction of the Spirit. "Lord, what wilt thou have me do?" (Acts 9:6). Jesus, you live in me, with your Father and your Holy Spirit (see Jn 14:23). "I live now not with my own life, but with the life of Christ who lives in me" (Gal 2:20).

To make my life over to Jesus, I have to follow his lead; I have to discern, that is, to look for and to know the different spirits that urge me to act: the Holy Spirit, the evil spirits, my own spirit.

St. John says, "Do not believe every spirit, but test the spirits to see whether they are of God" (1 Jn 4:1). It is in prayer, especially in contemplative prayer, that we come to know, to discern, what the Holy Spirit wills.

The discernment of spirits is always in and through love, the love that is poured into my heart through the Holy Spirit (Rom 5:5). The gift of love, the gift that the Father and Jesus give me in my heart through their Spirit, empowers me to love, raises up and enriches my capacity to love.

This gift of love enables me to enter into contemplation, that is, to look with the eyes of faith at the Lord, to keep my eyes fixed on Jesus. Because contemplation is knowledge through love.

Discernment, the discernment of spirits, is judgment based on knowledge through love. The judgment is always made in and through love.

We can learn about love and about discernment of spirits from St. Paul's first Letter to the Corinthians. They had a lot of problems in the city of Corinth, and that was the reason Paul wrote to them. Their biggest problem was that they lacked love; lacking love, they lacked discernment, and lacking discernment, they made several bad judgments and evaluations, and so fell into quite serious difficulties. The Corinthians did not seem to know that Christian knowledge is knowledge through love. St. Paul's first letter to them is an effort to straighten out their thinking and acting.

Judging from the letter, the Christians at Corinth put a high value on certain gifts of the Spirit, especially the gifts of knowledge, wisdom, prophesying in tongues, and any gift that seemed to manifest mysterious and hidden knowledge. They really had gifts of the Holy Spirit, and Paul thanks God that they are "enriched in him with all speech and all knowledge" (1 Cor 1:5). But he does not praise them for faith, hope, and love, as he does the other churches (see Rom 1:8; Col 1:4; 1 Thes 1:3). The Corinthians had charismatic gifts but not virtues; above all, they lacked love (see 1 Cor 13).

So the Corinthians were using the gifts of wisdom and knowledge in a worldly way, that is, without founding them on love. But "God has made foolish the wisdom of the world" (1:20). And "if I have ... all knowledge . . . but have not love, I am nothing" (13:2). So, Paul says, he cannot address them as spiritual men, but as men of the flesh (3:1). There is among them jealousy and strife. They lack unity, and the church is breaking down into factions—some for Paul, some for Apollos, some for Cephas (1:11-13; 3:3-23). They even seem divided over issues like whether or not women should wear veils in the assembly (11:2-16). And they bring lawsuits against one another in the civil courts (6:1-7). They wrong and defraud one another (6:8).

The Corinthians lack not only wisdom but basic prudence and common sense. At their celebration of the Lord's supper, "each one goes ahead with his own meal, and one is hungry and another is drunk" (11:21).

They seem to have serious problems with sexual

morality (6:13-20), and tolerate even incest (5:1-13). Some, it seems, frequent prostitutes (6:15).

The prayer assemblies apparently are chaotic, with many prophecies in tongues and few or no interpretations, even with several persons at a time prophesying in tongues (chapter 14). Anyone who has ever heard a prophecy in tongues at a pentecostal or charismatic prayer meeting can imagine the disorder in the Corinthians' meetings.

Furthermore, their gifts of speech and knowledge have made them arrogant, inflated their pride, made them puffed up (see 4:6,18; 5:2; 13:5). In light of all this, one might read Paul's description of love in chapter 13, verses 4 to 7, as a list of the Corinthians' fundamental defects: to be unkind, impatient, puffed up, selfish, bad-mannered, irritable, grudge-holding, lacking faith, lacking hope, and of course, lacking love.

The heart of the first Letter to the Corinthians is the thirteenth chapter. What the Corinthian Christians need and lack most is love. And Paul encourages them to pray for the charisms, but above all to pray for love. Love is more than a charism. It is a way—a way of life, a road, a life pathway (12:31). And without love the charisms are nothing. Clearly, Paul wants the Christians at Corinth to make the application to the gifts of knowledge and wisdom for which he praised them early in the letter. Knowledge not informed by love is nothing; wisdom not in Christian love is only worldly wisdom, if that; every gift must be used in love, informed by love.

Lacking love, the Corinthians do not know through love, and so their knowledge is wrong and wrongheaded. Lacking love, they make judgments and decisions not in love but in selfishness and pride and resentment, and so their wisdom is not Christian.

Lacking true knowledge, they fail to exercise Christian discernment, which is knowledge through love. And lacking discernment, they choose wrongly and fall into all the problems that Paul points at in the letter.

Love is the basis for discernment. Discernment enables me to "walk as he walked" (1 Jn 2:6), to "walk in the light" (1 Jn 1:7).

Prayer for the gift of love:

Lord Jesus, give me the gift of love.
Teach me to walk always in that way which is the love that you pour into my heart. Lead me always along the path that is the love you give me through the gift of your Holy Spirit.

Teach me to know you always better and better through the love that you pour into my heart through your Spirit. Teach me to pray contemplatively. And guide me all through every day so that I walk always with my eyes on you. Let me walk always in your Spirit.

Teach me, Jesus, discernment. Give me and increase in me the gift of listening to your voice, of being able to tell what is your voice from what is not. Make me sensitive and docile to the urgings that come from your Spirit. Let me walk always in your Spirit. Amen.

Making Decisions

If I am trying to "walk by the Spirit," as St. Paul urges (Gal 5:16), then I want every decision I make, small or large, to have its foundation in my relationship with the Lord. In the light of his love shall I do this or shall I do that? It matters to him because he loves me, and his love has plans for me. But if I do not have a regular prayer life and even regular contemplation in my life, I will not have the necessary relationship with the Lord for truly discerning, recognizing what decisions are the ones he wants me to make.

Different spirits influence me: the good Spirit, that is, God speaking to me through his Holy Spirit—"Thou gavest thy good Spirit to instruct them" (Neh 9:20); evil spirits; or my own disordered inclinations, such as pride, worldliness, prejudices, or even my likes and dislikes, my fears.

Unless I put in time regularly and faithfully contemplating the Lord, I will hardly be able to have the kind of face-to-face relationship I need with him in order to discern which of these spirits is moving me. But if I do give my life over to Jesus—"In him we live and move and have our being," says St. Paul (Acts 17:28)—then I can count on God, for Jesus told us, "The Holy Spirit, whom the Father will send in my name, he will teach you all things" (Jn 14:26).

The steps in making a decision begin with collecting all the facts and relevant information, perhaps taking advice. I weigh the pros and cons. I look into my own heart after asking the Lord's light and guidance. The Book of Proverbs observes that "the purpose in a man's mind is like deep water, but a man of understanding will draw it out," and "the spirit of man is the lamp of the Lord, searching all his innermost parts" (Prv 20:5, 27). I need a free heart to sift things out.

The second step is to take the possible decisions to the Lord in prayer. It is well to express the possible decision clearly as a question needing a yes or no. "Shall I apply for this job?" Hold the question up to the Lord in prayer. Look at him with faith and trust and love, quietly and simply, to find out which of the answers will be truly his. If it is an important decision, do this for some minutes (for example, twenty or thirty), or perhaps every day for a week or two for just a few minutes. Small decisions can be handled quickly. I try the yes answer and the no answer and find which feels most right in the framework of my love relationship with the Lord. After a time, or even right at the beginning and from then on, I will feel consolation with regard to one of the options. I will feel a consistent peace and interior harmony, a consoling rightness, or perhaps a real gladness and joy of heart. "The fruit of the Spirit is . . . joy, peace" (Gal 5:22). These are signs that the particular option is from the good Spirit.

So the decision is made. But can I be sure? I stay with the decision for some days, testing it, holding it up to the Lord for confirmation to see if it really is from him. If it is, the consolation will continue, even though the decision may be a painful one.

Group discernment.

If my decision involves others, I may need to pray with them. A husband and wife may need to come to a joint decision. In that case they will need to each discern individually, to pool the results of their prayerful discernment, and to pray together discerning. A family, a religious community, a business team, can discern together in prayer. Here are the general steps:

1. Collect, study, evaluate, and weigh the facts and factors impinging on the decision: One or a few people can do this for the group.

2. Pray together, listening to the Lord (in silence or with spontaneous prayer, or using the gifts of the Spirit, or however seems appropriate for the particular group, briefly.)

3. Discuss the matter, formulating the question simply and clearly.

4. Then each person prays on his or her own,

taking the question to the Lord (twenty or thirty minutes, for example).

5. Meet again; go around the circle, with each briefly giving the result of his or her prayer and how he or she has decided in prayer. Do not discuss; only say what happened.

6. Discuss again, this time in the light of the sharing.

7. Conclude and plan. Or, if necessary, split up and pray again, meet again, share, discuss, conclude, and plan.

Prayer:

Lord Jesus, teach me your ways. Teach me to walk always in your Holy Spirit. With the help of your grace, I ask that all my choices be in accord with my basic choice of you as my Savior. I ask that all my decisions, the daily quickly made ones and the important decisions of my life, be made in accord with the loving plan you have for me. Amen.

THREE

Praying with the Bible

This gate is the Lord's;
the just shall enter by it. (Ps 118:20)

T HE LORD'S GATE IS THE BIBLE, the word of God. Because the Bible is God's inspired word, it brings us to God's divine Word, to Jesus our Savior.

Psalms of Praise

The sections in this chapter do not deal with reading the Bible, nor even with understanding it. The subject here is praying the Bible, using Bible passages in prayer.

One way to use the Bible in your daily prayer is this: You can take a psalm and read it very slowly. Read a verse or a phrase, and then stop. Put the Bible aside. Just rest there in and with that phrase or verse, in calm and in peace, in the presence of the Lord and knowing he loves you. Then, after a while, go on to the next phrase or to the next verse. Read that slowly.

Then rest there with it, looking at the Lord with the eyes of faith, remaining quietly attentive to the Lord, resting in the tone or the spirit or the basic fact of the phrase or verse you have read.

The point here is not thinking but looking. Do not meditate or think about the phrase or ruminate its meaning for your own life. Rather, look at the Lord. The Bible verse is a point of reference. But the focus of your prayer is not the Bible verse; it is the Lord. Instead of thinking, just still your mind and look at the Lord. This prayer is an easy kind of contemplation, of looking in faith at the Lord. It is a way to know the Lord through love. Not intellectually and not in the way you can know about the Lord through studying the Bible—this kind of prayer is not Bible study. It is knowing the Lord through love. It is a prayer in the heart, not in the head. It is a loving look at the Lord, a looking in love, a quiet, loving, contemplative attention to him.

Psalms of praise.
For example, let us take the psalms of praise and see how we might use them in prayer. Basically, there are two kinds of psalms: psalms of praise and psalms of petition and lament. These two categories—praise and petition—correspond to the two most basic ways of relating prayerfully to the Lord. All the other ways of relating to God can be reduced in some way to these two—plea and praise. Here we will take just the psalms of praise, and we will take up the psalms of petition and lament in the following section.

It might help to know that the psalms of praise have a definite structure. This structure depends for its form on the kind of praise. There are psalms where the individual praises God by describing what God has done for him—for example, Psalms 18, 30, 40, and 66. Praise in these psalms is close to thanksgiving. The psalm takes the form of a kind of thanksgiving for having been rescued or saved in some way, and it has this form:

1. I remember when I was in trouble.
2. I cried out to the Lord.
3. He heard me.
4. And he saved me.

The other kind of praise psalm is the psalm that praises the Lord by describing his greatness and goodness. These are, then, psalms that describe not so much what God has done for you individually but how good and great he is. These psalms do not have the same unity of structure as do the psalms that are prayers of the individual praising God for his mercies toward that individual. They usually begin with a call to praise. Then the psalm goes on to praise God himself, or perhaps for his creation, or for what he has done for his people. There are many of these: for example, Psalms 95, 100, 145, 148, and 150; also, Psalms 135, 136, 146, and 147; and of course many others.

Praying with a psalm of praise.

To whom should I pray when I am praying with a psalm? I can use the psalm to pray to Jesus, to unite me more closely with him. After reading a phrase or verse, I can rest in quiet and loving attention to Jesus, looking at him with the eyes of faith. Or I can go with Jesus to the Father. The psalms are prayers that Jesus knew and used in praying to the Father. I can unite myself with Jesus and go with him to the Father. After reading a verse or a phrase of the psalm, I look with Jesus at the Father, with love and in faith.

Here are two examples:

Praying a psalm to Jesus.
Come before Jesus; kneel or sit or stand—whatever best expresses your prayer. If you are alone, you could use gestures to pray.

Psalm 138: I give thee thanks, O Lord,
with my whole heart;

Look at Jesus, not with imagination but with the reality of faith. Maybe lift up your hands. Look at him with love. That word *thee*, which sounds old-fashioned in English, is really the tender, loving word that other languages still use to speak to children and very close friends. It expresses tender love, and gratitude—as much as we will feel when we see Jesus in heaven and realize who he is. Pray very slowly, maybe repeating the phrase.

Before the heavens I sing thy praise;

We do not know the words of the ineffable praise, but join in, just singing in jubilation—in words, in tongues, or just in your heart. Rest quietly then, knowing you are part of the heavenly chorus with Mary, the angels, and the saints.

I bow down toward thy holy temple

Do that: bow down before Jesus seated at the right hand of God the Father and enthroned within you, because "Do you not know that your body is a temple of the Holy Spirit within you, which you have from God?" (1 Cor 6:19). A bodily prayer.

And give thanks to thy name

Repeat very slowly the holy name of Jesus—just savor it—the "name which is above every name, that at the name of Jesus every knee should bow" (Phil 2:9-10).

for thy steadfast love and thy faithfulness.

This phrase will melt your heart—stay there. If you have been unfaithful, unloving, just put that into the steadfast, loving heart of Jesus, with wordless sorrow. We never come before Jesus, or look at him, without receiving love, mercy, grace and strength. When the woman touched the hem of his garment, Jesus said, "Somebody touched me. I felt that power had gone out from me" (Lk 8:46). "Everyone in the crowd was trying to touch him because power came out of him that cured them all" (Lk 6:19).

One should not worry about completing the psalm. Stay where you find fruit.

Praying a psalm with Jesus to the Father.

A number of Scripture passages speak of Jesus at prayer. But Hebrews 7:25 tells us that Jesus is still praying in heaven: "He is living for ever to intercede for all who come to God through him." So this is a very important way to pray. We place ourselves with Jesus and pray with him—maybe as a small child prays with his mother, not comprehending fully; maybe as a son of God with the Son (see Gal 4:7). Always we come in awe and love.

> Psalm 103: Bless the Lord, O my soul;
> and all that is within me,
> bless his holy name!

This is truly the prayer of Jesus: "Father, hallowed be thy name." Let Jesus make the prayer—it is too ineffable for us. Just give him all that is within you.

> Bless the Lord, O my soul,
> and forget not all his benefits,

Jesus, we know, loved the leper who came back to

thank him, and he looked around for the other nine. So thanking is important to Jesus. He alone knows how much thanks we owe the Father for all his benefits to us. Let Jesus express it fully. Feel the happiness of being able to thank adequately, through Jesus.

who forgives all your iniquity,

Can Jesus pray this with us? Yes, because "for our sake God made the sinless one into sin, so that in him we might become the goodness of God" (2 Cor 5:21). "He was bearing our faults in his own body on the cross" (1 Pt 2:24). He alone knows the heinousness of those sins which he became, which he nailed to the cross in his body—sin before the holiness of his Father. Stay close to Jesus as he makes our act of contrition with us, then open your heart and your life and your world to receive the holiness, the goodness of God, which Jesus obtained for us in exchange for our sin.

Continue the psalm with Jesus as he prays with and for you. Again, do not try to finish; stop wherever you can pray even wordlessly, just looking with Jesus at our Father, quietly, in faith.

Psalms of Lament

In the previous section we looked at psalms of praise. Here we consider psalms of lament and how we might use them in our prayer.

The pattern that many of these psalms follow reflects the way we instinctively pray to God when we are suffering. Usually they begin with *a cry to God*:

> My God, my God. (Ps 22:1)
> Save me, O God! (Ps 69:1)
> Have mercy on me, O God. (Ps 51:1)
> O God, why dost thou cast us off forever?
>   (Ps 74:11)
> Out of the depths I cry to thee, O Lord!
>   (Ps 130:1)
> As a hart longs
>   for flowing streams,
> so longs my soul
>   for thee, O God. (Ps 42:1)
> Hear my prayer, O Lord. (Ps 143:1)

Then the psalmist *tells God in detail what his trouble is.* It could be one of the following laments:

> I pour out my complaint before him;
>   I tell my trouble before him. (Ps 142:2)
> Why hast thou forsaken me? (Ps 22:1)
> Ruthless men seek my life. (Ps 54:3)
> My heart is in anguish within me,
>   the terrors of death have fallen upon me.
>   (Ps 55:4)
> . . . those who would destroy me . . . attack
>   me with lies.
> What I did not steal
>   must I now restore? (Ps 69:4)

Thou hast made the land to quake,
   thou hast rent it open. (Ps 60:2)
Thy hand has come down on me.
   There is no soundness in my flesh. (Ps 38:2-3)
For the waters have come up to my neck.
   I sink in deep mire. (Ps 69:1-2)

Having cried out and lamented, the psalm-prayer always *trusts*. The psalmist says he will cling to God, even if he feels no better. But with confidence he urges his cause:

Wake up, Lord. Why are you asleep? (Ps 44:23)
I wait for the Lord, my soul waits,
   and in his word I hope. (Ps 130:5)
I know that the Lord maintains the
   cause of the afflicted,
and executes justice for the needy. (Ps 140:12)
Yet God my King is from of old,
   working salvation in the midst of the earth.
   (Ps 74:12)
Why are you cast down, O my soul,
   and why are you disquieted within me?
Hope in God . . . my help and my God. (Ps 42:5-6)

Confidence crystallizes in *petition*. The extreme distress is still there, but not despair. Trust is calmer, though urgent, as the psalmist asks:

Hasten to my aid! (Ps 22:19)
Let not . . . the pit close its mouth over me.
   (Ps 69:15)

> Send out thy light and thy truth; let them lead me.
>   (Ps 43:3)
> At an acceptable time, O God,
>   in the abundance of thy steadfast
>   love answer me.
> With thy faithful help rescue me
>   from sinking in the mire;
> let me be delivered from my enemies. (Ps 69:13)
> Bring me out of prison. (Ps 142:7)
> In thy righteousness bring me out of trouble!
>   (Ps 143:11)
> O God my Lord,
>   deal on my behalf for thy name's sake. . . .
> For I am poor . . .
>   my heart is stricken. (Ps 109:21-22)
> O my God, . . . take me not hence
>   in the midst of my days. (Ps 102:24)

The psalm of lament cries out, complains, trusts, asks. Usually the conclusion is *a promise of thanks and praise*; often too, *a promise to give witness* to the way the Lord rescues and saves.

> My tongue will sing aloud of thy deliverance.
>   (Ps 51:14)
> So will I ever sing praises to thy name. (Ps 61:8)
> I will magnify him with thanksgiving. (Ps 69:30)
> My lips will shout for joy,
>   when I sing praises to thee;
>   my soul also, which thou hast rescued.

And my tongue will talk of thy righteous help
   all the day long. (Ps 71:23-24)
With my mouth I will give great thanks
   to the Lord;
I will praise him in the midst of the throng.
For he stands at the right hand of the needy.
   (Ps 109:30-31)

Praying a psalm of lament with Jesus.
Did Jesus pray the psalms of lament? Can we pray
this way with him? Scripture tells us that Jesus
"offered prayers and supplications with loud cries
and tears" (Heb 5:7). Jesus was lamenting to God.
As he hung on the cross, the bystanders heard
snatches of his prayer. It was Psalm 22: "My God, my
God, why have you deserted me?" Jesus was
lamenting, complaining, reproaching his heavenly
Father—yet with loving reverence. "He offered
prayers and supplications with loud cries and tears
to God, who was able to save him from death, and he
was heard because of his reverence" (Heb 5:7).

Jesus on the cross, praying Psalm 22, described
his agony to his Father:

Why have you deserted me? . . .
I call all day, my God, but you never answer,
all night long I call and cannot rest. . . .
Here am I now more worm than man. . . .
All who see me jeer at me. . . .

My bones are all disjointed,
my heart is like wax, melting inside me; . . .
my tongue is stuck to my jaw.

Jesus offered up all his trust:

Yet, Holy One, . . .
in you our fathers put their trust . . .
never in vain.
They called to you for help and they were saved.

Jesus made his petition:

Come quickly to my help; . . .
rescue my soul, . . . my dear life.

Jesus knew he had to undergo death. God's help would not take him down from the cross but would raise him out of death. Praying Psalm 22, he ended with a promise of praise and of witness:

Then I shall proclaim your name to my brothers,
praise you in full assembly.

Some psalms of lament particularly suitable for personal prayer are Psalms 22, 42, 44, 69, 88, 102, and 140. Choose one of these psalms and pray your way through it, going slowly, as slowly as possible. Stay with the same phrase or verse as long as you find fruit there, as long as you can, so to speak, relish the words, as long as you feel at peace there and somehow in relationship with God. Do not pray with many words, but rest quietly with a phrase of the psalm, looking silently at God with the eyes of faith. You probably will not finish the psalm. But the point, of course, is not to finish but to be quietly with the Lord.

The Prodigal Son

One way to use a gospel passage for prayer is to put myself in the place of the person who is healed or forgiven or chosen by Jesus. In this way, I can apply the passage to myself and, in prayer, enter into a loving and trusting relationship with Jesus in terms of his saving relation to me. I can take the role of Peter, or of Mary Magdalene, or of Zacchaeus, or of a leper or a blind man who cries out to Jesus for healing. And I can go to the Lord on those terms. Or I can understand myself as the central figure in one of the parables. I am the barren fig tree that the Lord gives still more time to bear fruit; I am the man to whom the Lord gives certain talents that are to be used; I am the lost sheep and the lost coin; I am, for Jesus, the kingdom, the treasure hidden in a field, a pearl of great price.

Let us take one gospel passage, the parable of the prodigal son, and pray our way through the story, identifying with the prodigal son. I am the prodigal son; you are the prodigal son.

The prodigal son has sinned and, in fact, has gotten his life in a serious mess. He is miserable; his survival is at stake. He has lost everything: his money, his good clothes, his friends. He is alone except for the pigs. The pigs symbolize his sins and his problems. Worst of all, and most profoundly, *the prodigal son has lost his dignity as a human being.*

He repents. His repentance remains at a low level: mainly, he wants to get out of the mess he has made of his life. But his repentance is sincere, real. It involves, necessarily, the renunciation of his present state in the pigpen. He renounces the pigs and the pen; he renounces his sins and his whole sorry condition.

And so can we. Let us pray together slowly and sincerely:

Lord Jesus, I renounce my sin. I renounce the devil and all his works. I renounce worldly values and the false glamour of sin. Jesus, I renounce all pride and arrogance and my vanity, which desires esteem and attention. I renounce envy. I renounce all anger, all resentment, all unforgiveness; give me a forgiving heart, compassionate and ready to forgive. I renounce all greediness and every spirit of avarice. I renounce every spirit of lust and all sinfulness in the area of my sexuality. I renounce the spirit and every sin of gluttony. And I renounce all sloth, especially the spiritual sloth that keeps me from running to you. *Free me, Lord*

Jesus. Jesus, free me. I renounce all anxiety, all fear and timidity, the spirit of scrupulosity, and every spirit of sadness and depression. I renounce any false and objectively unjustified feeling of guilt. And I renounce all self-hatred and rejection of myself, all dislike of myself. *Free me, Lord Jesus.*

The prodigal son returns to his father. No matter what state I am in—a bad one (chronic sin or habits of sin, drug or alcohol problems, bitterness, anguish) or not so bad (lack of love for the Lord and for other persons, tepidity in my spiritual life, coldness of heart, impatience, unkindness, always committing the same faults and sins)—I can return to my heavenly Father. Jesus guides me; I go with him.

The prodigal son makes plans. He wants to improve, to change his life. He will return to his father's farm, humbly. "Father," he plans to say, "I have sinned against heaven and against you; make me one of your hired servants." His repentance is still imperfect: he plans to bargain, although humbly, with his father. I can cry out to my Father even though my repentance remains far from perfect.

Father, heavenly Father, please let me serve you faithfully from now on. You know I am not yet wholly willing to give up my sin. Help me, Father.

The son has reckoned without his prodigal father, a

father prodigal in love and forgiveness. The father sees his son coming a long way off. "His father saw him and was moved with pity. He ran to the boy, clasped him in his arms, and kissed him" (Lk 15:20). The father does not speak. He just embraces his son. And in that embrace the son's human dignity is restored. The father's embrace forgives the son and heals his hurts. "The son said, 'Father, I have sinned against heaven and against you. I no longer deserve to be called your son'" (Lk 15:21). The son does not bargain now. "I will earn my keep in your service" (Make me one of your hired servants). His father's embrace brings him to true sorrow: "I have sinned. . . . I am no longer worthy to be your son." Let us pray together slowly to our heavenly Father.

Father, I come to you with Jesus. I see you, Father, on the road ahead of me, running toward me. Father, I have sinned against heaven and against you; I do not deserve to be called your child. Father, you are embracing me, holding me. I accept your forgiveness. I accept your love for me. I accept the healing you are giving me. I accept the new dignity and worth you make me feel. I am happy to be your child. Abba, Father, there was never a more miserable sinner than I. I have known your love, but I chose to leave you and to waste the life and the love you have given me, going my way instead of yours. Father, my sorrow is inadequate; but with the little I have, I come to you. I cannot keep the resolutions I make; I need power other than my own. Father, Jesus reveals you to me; he shares you with me. I come to you now in Jesus. Lift me up, Father, please take me back. I accept all your love for me now. I know my own weakness and the reservations I make. But I cry out to you; I run into your arms. Take me into your arms, into your heart. Give me all I need—the garment of grace, the ring of belonging to you, the sandals to walk in your Holy Spirit. Lead me to the party of your joy in me. Let me join in the music and dancing of your delight in me, of your delight in forgiving me and in taking me back. I have been dead; you bring me back to life. I have been lost; you have found me. Amen.

"I Have Called You by Name, You Are Mine"

God speaks to his people Israel in the Old Testament through the prophets. He inspires the Old Testament prophets to speak God's word—his word of admonition, his word of love, his word of consolation. In the New Testament now, God speaks his Word-become-flesh, Jesus. Jesus is God's Word to all of us and to each of us. What does God, in and through Jesus, say to you and to me? What does Jesus say to you and to me?

Jesus speaks to each of us the same message that the Old Testament prophets communicated to Israel. In fact, I can take many of the Old Testament prophecies and hear Jesus speaking to me personally. I can apply them to myself as the word of the Lord to me personally.

The Lord says to me now, "I have called you by name, you are mine" (Is 43:1).

Reflection.

When Mary Magdalene encountered Jesus after his resurrection, she spoke with him without recognizing him. But then he said to her, "Mary" (see Jn 20:11-18). She had thought he was the gardener, but as he called her by name, she knew him. When we go to meet Jesus in prayer, Jesus speaks our name, and we know him, we love him. Jeremiah the prophet could never resist the Lord who had called him. The Lord had told Jeremiah: "Before I formed you in the womb I knew you" (Jer 1:5). Sometimes, when his speaking the word of the Lord brought him into trouble and suffering, Jeremiah tried not to hear the Lord calling him by name, but he could not. "You have seduced me, Yahweh, and I have let myself be seduced" (Jer 20:7). God speaks my name, calling me, calling me to a transforming experience of Jesus, to a loving personal relationship with Jesus.

To be called by name is to be chosen. With all possible creation before him, God decided, in love, to create me. He called out my name, and I came into being. "*Before* I formed you in the womb I knew you." With all people on earth assembled before him, God chose me in a special way—called out my name—as one chosen to know him, to praise, reverence, and serve him.

Jesus said to the disciples, "Rejoice that your names are written in heaven" (Lk 10:20). The Book of Revelation speaks of those whose names were "written before the foundation of the world in the book of life" (see Rv 13:8). So precious are we to Jesus our Savior that he promises to speak our names to his Father: "He who conquers shall be clad thus in white garments, and I will not blot his name out of the book of life; I will confess his name before my Father and before his angels" (Rv 3:5). But God said to Moses, "Whoever has sinned against me, him will I blot out of my book" (Ex 32:33).

As we remain quietly before Jesus, perhaps lovingly speaking *his* name as he speaks ours, we need to be open to him in those areas of our lives where we know we are not conquering, where we know we have no victory over ourselves. "Only the Holy Spirit can penetrate and win over to God certain areas of our lives and depths of our being where no divine commandment or evangelical counsel or ecclesiastical rule or personal resolution can reach" (Divarka, *Alive To God* [Rome: Centrum Ignatianum Spiritualitatis, 1979], p. 43).

Jesus has the victory. He can only effect it in us if we spend time with him, keep close to him. God revealed his own name to Moses: "The Lord whose name is Jealous" (Ex 34:14). "I am jealous for Zion with great jealousy, and I am jealous for her with great wrath" (Zec 8:2). His is a wrath against the forces of evil: "No one is able to snatch them out of the Father's hand" (Jn 10:29).

When we have appropriated the victory that Jesus won for us, have fought the good fight, and finally stand before him, he has made us a promise: "To him who conquers . . . I will give a white stone with a new name written on the stone which no one knows except him who receives it" (Rv 2:17). That is God's secret yet: the name by which he calls me. "I have called you by name, you are mine."

Prayer.
I can simply remain in silence, my mind and heart quite quiet, resting with the Lord, letting him call me personally by name, letting my response to his call be one of quiet loving attention to him-calling-me-to-himself. Or I can pray slowly and simply in my own words, telling the Lord how I feel, thanking him for his personal call to me, asking for the grace to respond to his call lovingly, generously, faithfully.

Or I can read Psalm 139 very slowly. It begins, "O Lord, thou hast searched me and known me! Thou knowest when I sit down and when I rise up; thou discernest my thoughts." The psalm can be made a loving prayer response to the Lord, an acknowledgment of his knowing me through and through, and a response to his love.

Lord Jesus, you call me by name. Help me to hear you call my name.

Help me to listen to you in silent love.
Teach me to be with you quietly in prayer.
Teach me to open my heart to your love and to
respond to the immense love you have for me.
Amen.

The Annunciation

There are various ways to use a Scripture text in
your personal prayer. The best way is to read the text
slowly, and then look at the Lord with the eyes of
faith to see how he leads you in prayer. He might
lead you just to himself, to simply be there with him,
in loving attention to him. Or he might lead you to
rest quietly with the text you have just read, savoring
it in his presence—"Taste and see that the Lord is
good." Or he could lead you to think about the
passage.

For example, the passage about the Annunciation,
Luke 1:26-28, can be used for personal prayer. Here
is a written reflection to read over and perhaps
meditate on, as you feel the Holy Spirit leads you.
The reflection is followed by some suggestions for
your prayer, some ways that you might relate to the
Lord in terms of the Annunciation passage.

Reflection.
If you ever go to Florence, in Italy, and visit the
monastery of San Marco, you will see that Fra
Angelico, who was a Dominican friar there, painted
a fresco in each cell and in all the rooms used by the

community. He painted the Annunciation twice: one fresco is at the head of the stairs, the other is in the third cell. There is a subtle but profound difference between the two, conveyed by the eyes and the stance of the figures. In the fresco in the cell, the angel is the dominant figure: he, Gabriel, is standing; Mary, the girl of Nazareth, is kneeling. The angel's eyes are a little puzzled, appraising. Mary's eyes are frankly worried—"She was greatly troubled," Luke tells us (Lk 1:29). In the other painting—a moment later— the scene is reversed. Mary is seated, and her eyes are full of wonder; the angel is in the act of genuflecting. Just to look at Mary, one knows that the Incarnation has come to be.

At the Annunciation, God "did not despise the virgin's womb," that is, he did not despise our humanity, did not despise becoming one of us. The Incarnation: "In the beginning was the Word, . . . and the Word was God. . . . And the Word became flesh" (Jn 1:1, 14). God became a fetus. The Annunciation: "Behold, I bring you good news of a great joy which will come to all the people" (Lk 2:10).

On coming into the world on the day of his Incarnation, God chose for himself the worst parts of our human life. To all appearances he was conceived out of wedlock, an illegitimate son of an unmarried mother. The baby was born in a shed, among animals. He was a displaced person, of a family escaping in fear of their lives from their own country, then living as refugees in a strange land. He belonged to a working-class family who earned their way in the uncertain trade of carpentry.

Then there was Jesus' personal struggle—"tempted as we are in all things (or 'in every way' NEB) yet without sinning" (Heb 4:15). His personal struggle reached a crisis in the Garden of Gethsemane: "Father, not that way ... but yes, as you want it" (see Mt 26:39), an echo of his mother's "Let it be to me according to your word" (Lk 1:38). So "for our sake God made the sinless one *into sin*" (2 Cor 5:21). There followed the betrayal, the desertion by his friends, the rigged trial, the imprisonment, torture, and finally execution. How low can life bring us and we not find that Jesus has been there before us, is there to meet us?

Jesus in his Incarnation chose the bitter things of our life. But there was one exception. He chose the best parents—Mary and his foster father Joseph. This shows us God's priorities.

Mary, in the moment of the Annunciation, put herself at God's disposal: "Behold the handmaid of the Lord" (Lk 1:38). God, taking her at her word, made her the mother not only of his divine Son but of each of us. Jesus is "the first-born among many brethren" (Rom 8:29). St. Paul says, and his words could have been spoken by Mary, "My little children, with whom I am again in travail until Christ be formed in you" (Gal 4:19).

What can we learn from our mother in the Annunciation? We can learn to have a family likeness to her and to our elder brother Jesus. We can learn to put ourselves at God's disposal: "Behold the handmaid of the Lord; be it done to me according to thy word" (Lk 1:38). "The Son of God, Jesus Christ, ... was not Yes and No; but in him it is always Yes" (2 Cor 1:19).

Suggestions for prayer.
If something in the above reflection struck you, go back to that and dwell on it. You could talk to the Lord about it: ask him to show you how it applies to your own life, to your relationship with him, to your relationships with others. You could ask the Lord for any particular graces you feel led to ask for, such as the grace to always respond positively to the Lord, to always say to him, "Yes, be it done unto me according to your word."

Or you might feel more comfortable with the Lord just resting in him in a silent attitude of gratitude or of love or of quiet peace in him.

Or, if you wish, you could pray very slowly, with long pauses, along these lines:

Mary, my mother, I come to you with trust, with much confidence in your goodness and in your love for me. Thank you for being my mother in heaven. Thank you for being the mother of Jesus, and of Jesus-in-my-life.

With you I want to say yes to God. I want to say, "Be it done to me according to your divine plan for my life." You said your yes to the angel at the Annunciation. You repeated it, saying yes to the flight into Egypt, saying yes at the wedding feast of Cana, saying yes to the Father at the foot of the cross. Help me to say yes to God. Help me to say yes to the graces he offers me, and especially to his gift of the Holy Spirit.

Jesus, I come to you with your mother Mary, with the mother you gave to me when you said from the cross, "Behold your mother." I come to you with Mary, my heavenly mother.

And I ask you for the gift of always saying yes to you and to the Father. I say yes to you now—yes to your love for me, to your guidance, to your care for me, to your Holy Spirit in my life—yes to you. Lord Jesus, you are my yes to the Father. In you, through you, with you, I say yes to the Father.

God my Father, I come to you with Jesus. You love me so much that you call me by name to come to you. You love me so much that you sent your Son Jesus to become human for me, to have Mary for his mother, to be persecuted and to suffer and die for me so that I could be fully your child, happy with you now, and happy with you forever in the world to come. In Jesus, and through him, and with him, I say yes to you. Amen. Amen. Amen. Our Father, who art in heaven, hallowed be thy name. . . .

Magnifying the Lord

Jesus "rejoiced in the Holy Spirit and said, 'I thank thee, Father, Lord of heaven and earth . . . '" (Lk 10:21). This beautiful trinitarian prayer is one of the few prayers of Jesus recorded in the Gospels. We know that Jesus prayed at Lazarus's tomb, "Father, I thank you for having heard me. I know that you always hear me" (Jn 11:41-42). And he teaches us to pray in his prayer to the Father, "Father, hallowed be thy name ..." (see Lk 11:2-4). We can join Jesus in saying these prayers, perhaps when we cannot find words or do not know how to approach God.

The Old Testament too has prayers that we can use: Abraham's servant prays for a wife for Isaac (Gn 24:12-14). Jacob prays to be protected from his brother, who might kill him (Gn 32:10-12). Moses prays that God will stay with his people even though they are sinful (Ex 34:9). Hannah prays to have a child (1 Sm 1:10-11). Solomon prays for the gift of discernment and wisdom in order to do the work the Lord has given him (1 Kgs 3:6-9).

At night prayer (Compline) the church uses the prayer of Zechariah, "Blessed be the Lord God ..." (see Lk 1:68-79). At evening prayer (Vespers) we use Our Lady's prayer, the Magnificat. If we want to pray the Magnificat with Mary, it is a good idea to use a translation that makes sense to us, that helps us to pray.

We can stand with arms upraised as Our Lady probably did. This is both a Jewish and an early Christian way of praying. Or we can kneel or sit— praying with body, mind, and heart, in whatever way best expresses our prayer. We can begin by asking

Our Lady to allow us to share her prayer, to pray with us. Then, looking at our Father, or at the Holy Trinity, or at Jesus, we can pray the Magnificat (see Lk 1:46-55).

"My soul magnifies the Lord."
Just lift your heart to God. You do not necessarily have to feel anything—though the gift of praise and the gift of worship are great graces. It is enough that we know that God is a wonder beyond all wonders, inexpressibly holy, beauty itself. Enough to say with Mary: "My soul magnifies you, O my God." If you have the gift of praise, let it flow. If you cannot find words, sing in tongues. Worship can be silent, but praise usually needs expression: "Holy, holy holy..." "Worthy is the Lamb... to receive... glory and blessing!" (Rv 4:8; 5:12).

Make yourself like a magnifying glass, transparent, letting the light of the Lord fill you and shine through you. Let the Lord and his love and his glory be magnified in and through you, like a magnifying glass of God. After praising the Lord, just be, magnifying the Lord with Mary, in silence; stay that way as long as it seems right and comfortable with the Lord.

"My spirit rejoices in God my Savior." (v. 47)
Let your heart rejoice in God for himself. Tell the Lord that. Then thank him for being Savior as well as

God. Rejoice that you are saved. God has been for eternity. He was waiting for the moment in time when he would become man, live, die. Why? To save me! No wonder my inmost spirit can rejoice in such a God.

Rejoice with the angels, together with your guardian angel and with Mary, Queen of Angels. You can sing quietly, "Rejoice in the Lord always; again I say Rejoice." Or, "This is the day that the Lord has made; let us rejoice and be glad in it." Perhaps sing in tongues again, with gladness in the Lord. Angels are singing with you. And Our Lady.

"He has regarded the low estate of his handmaiden." (v. 48)

At the visitation to Elizabeth, Mary—conceived without sin and carrying God-made-human in her womb—knows her lowliness, recognizes her smallness. She knows that her very littleness and weakness make her attractive to God. The Lord leaves the ninety-nine sheep to look for the one lost. He delights more in his returned prodigal child than in the one who stayed at home. He loves each of us with great compassion—a compassion that goes out lovingly to your weakness, your sinfulness, your inability to pray. He loves you because of these, not in spite of them. They are a share in his cross. His loving mercy can be magnified in and through the magnifying glass of your problems, sinfulness, fragility, littleness, difficulties. Give all that to the

Lord, who says, "Come to me, all who labor and are heavy laden" (Mt 11:28). With Mary, rest quietly, lowly and humble, like Jesus: "Learn from me; for I am gentle and lowly in heart" (Mt 11:29).

"Henceforth all generations will call me blessed." (v. 48)

Can you say this with Our Lady? Yes, you can apply it to yourself. Who would not envy you who know and draw near to the living God? "Blessed are you who are called to his supper." "Blessed are you poor, for yours *is* the kingdom of God" (Lk 6:20). "Come, O blessed of my Father..." (Mt 25:34). "Blessed are those who have not seen and yet believe" (Jn 20:29).

"He who is mighty has done great things for me." (v. 49)

Our Lady prays this uniquely. But you can thank God for the great things, and the *specific* things, you have seen him do in your life, and for his plan for your future, for being your future.

"Holy is his name." (v. 49)

The Lord might touch you with the awe of his holiness. Or you might be more active, for example, singing quietly a song: "Blessed Be the Name," or "Holy, Holy, Lord God Almighty." Or say the "Holy, Holy, Holy" from the Mass liturgy, reciting it slowly and pausing after words or phrases. Or just praise the Lord in your own language or in tongues.

"Mercy on those who fear him . . . as he spoke to our fathers." (vv. 50-55)

These next few lines of Mary's prayer praise the Lord's plan of action: his mercy, his power to save those who know they are needy, his rejection of the proud who think they are self-sufficient, his love of the poor and downtrodden, his judgment on those who ignore or trample on their neighbors. This is still, after two thousand years, a description of contemporary society in many parts of the world. It calls us to action as well as to prayer of intercession.

In verses 54-55 Our Lady, true Jew and first to find her Jewish heritage completed in Christ Jesus, Mary, the first Christian, praises Yahweh who has fulfilled the promises he made to Abraham, to all her ancestors. Now we too have been admitted to that heritage; we are children of Abraham. "You, my brothers [and sisters], like Isaac [Abraham's son], are children of the promise" (Gal 4:28). With Mary, thank the Lord for the goodness of his mercy in fulfilling his promise to you, his promise of love and blessing and salvation.

Conclusion.

Instead of concluding your prayer in a kind of closing down of your prayerfulness, extend it throughout the rest of the day. Take one thing from your prayer—a word (*mercy* or *holy*, for example) or a phrase ("My soul magnifies the Lord," or "Look on my lowliness")—that you can remember off and on during the day. That way, you can extend your prayer during your other daily activities. You might want to write the word or phrase on your calendar for that day, or on a slip of paper to leave on your desk or put in your pocket or purse, where you will find it whenever you put your hand in, and so be reminded to turn to the Lord. Magnify the Lord—with Mary—all day.

"Behold, the Lamb of God"

In praying with Scripture, I can take three quick preparatory steps before getting into the main part of my time with the Lord.

First, I recognize God's presence. I make myself conscious of the reality of Jesus' loving presence to me here and now, in this place and at this time. I might even vocalize a prayer: "Lord Jesus, thank you for loving me; teach me to pray."

Second, I read the text that I have selected for my prayer. Often it will be the gospel of the day, or perhaps a psalm that has struck me recently, or a Scripture text that I feel the Lord has in some way given to me personally. I read the text slowly, in the Lord's loving presence, in reverence both for him and for his word in the text. In the present case, read John's Gospel, chapter 1, verses 24 to 34:

Now they [priests and Levites] had been sent from the Pharisees. They asked him [John the Baptist],

"Then why are you baptizing, if you are neither the Christ, nor Elijah, nor the prophet?" John answered them, "I baptize with water; but among you stands one whom you do not know, even he who comes after me, the thong of whose sandal I am not worthy to untie." This took place in Bethany beyond the Jordan, where John was baptizing.

The next day he saw Jesus coming toward him, and said, "Behold, the Lamb of God, who takes away the sin of the world! This is he of whom I said, 'After me comes a man who ranks before me, for he was before me.' I myself did not know him; but for this I came baptizing with water, that he might be revealed to Israel."

And John bore witness, "I saw the Spirit descend as a dove from heaven, and it remained on him. I myself did not know him; but he who sent me to baptize with water said to me, 'He on whom you see the Spirit descend and remain, this is he who baptizes with the Holy Spirit.' And I have seen and have borne witness that this is the Son of God."

Third, I ask for the grace I want from my prayer. Usually I ask always for the same grace. For example, *"Lord Jesus, teach me to know you better, so that I can love you more and follow you more closely."* Or I might adapt my prayer for the grace I want to the subject matter. If I am praying about the Passion, I can ask for the grace to enter more fully into Jesus' suffering, to feel some of his suffering and anguish and pain, to be with him in my heart as he suffers and dies for love of me. If I am praying about the Resurrection or one of Jesus' appearances after the Resurrection, I can ask for the grace to know Jesus better as my consoler, as the giver of hope and strength.

These three preliminary steps should not take long. After I make them, then I begin the main part of my prayer. Here I should go the way the Lord leads me. I remain at ease and flexible, the eyes of my heart on the Lord, and I go the way he indicates, the way he moves me. The Lord might move me into a quiet—perhaps dry and dark, or perhaps felt and happy—union with him. He might lead me to just quietly and without words sink into the Scripture text, and through the text to sink into his love, into him.

Or he might lead me to ponder slowly and in love, with him, the richness of the text. Here is a reflection to help you meditate on the text. Note, however, that the whole point of your prayer is *Jesus,* not thoughts or feelings about him. Stop where you find Jesus. Rest there in him. You may not need the "reflection" or "meditation" part. Better if you don't! But if you do, these thoughts might help. If you use them, take them very slowly.

Reflection on John 1:24-34:

Lord Jesus, you are the Lamb of God. You take

away the sins of the world. You take away my sins, my sinfulness, my resistance to you, my coldness of heart, my fears and worries and anxieties, my resentments, my feelings of guilt, my discouragement, whatever separates me from you. "Behold, the Lamb of God; behold him who takes away the sins of the world."

Lord Jesus, you were oppressed and you were afflicted, but you did not open your mouth. Like a lamb that they led to slaughter, like a sheep in the hands of its shearers, you did not open your mouth (see Is 53:7). Like a gentle lamb led to slaughter (see Jer 11:19), a lamb without spot or blemish (see 1 Pt 1:19), you went to your murder by torture. You did that for love of me. You gave yourself over as a sacrificial lamb, as an offering, as expiation and reparation for my sins and for my sinfulness. For love of me.

And now, Jesus, you carry the wounds in your body, in your hands and feet and side. Those wounds you suffered for me are now glorified, part of your risen and glorified body. Thank you, Jesus, for saving me. I want to thank you and praise you and adore you. You are the Lamb that was slain. I want to sing—with everyone in heaven—the "song of the Lamb" (see Rv 15:3-4).

Lord Jesus, I want to see you now with the eyes of faith, to humble myself before you, and to praise you and glorify you. "I saw a Lamb standing, as though it had been slain; . . . and they sang a new song, saying: 'Worthy art thou, . . . for thou wast slain and by thy blood didst ransom us for God from every tribe and tongue and people and nation, and hast made us a kingdom and priests to our God'" (Rv 5:6, 9-10).

Worthy are you, Jesus. You have been slain for me. Worthy are you to receive power and riches and wisdom and mightiness and honor and glory and blessing! To the Lamb be blessing and glory and honor and power for ever and ever! Amen! (see Rv 5:12-14).

Contemplative prayer.
Jesus, the Lamb of God, is with you, looking at you with love. Stay quietly in his presence, conscious of his loving gaze. Jesus is standing in front of you, loving you. Rest in his love. Be at peace, be with him.

Jesus Risen as Consoler

We have written about how to use Scripture texts in personal prayer. In this section we want to give you some ideas about praying with gospel texts that speak of Jesus' resurrection or of his post-resurrection appearances to his disciples.

The Resurrection texts are especially important because, of course, the Jesus who is with me in my personal prayer is Jesus risen. There are several of these texts, especially in the Gospels of John and Luke.

I can take for my personal prayer Luke 24:36-43, for example. I might use this same text for one day, or for several, or even for a week or so, until I am ready to move on to another text.

I begin my prayer at a time I have set, in a place where I can be quiet. And I follow three preliminary steps.

First step: recognizing the Lord's presence:
Lord Jesus, thank you for being here with me. Teach me to pray.

Second step: reading the text:
As they were saying this, Jesus himself stood among them. But they were startled and frightened, and supposed that they saw a spirit. And he said to them, "Why are you troubled, and why do questionings arise in your hearts? See my hands and my feet, that it is I myself; handle me, and see; for a spirit has not flesh and bones as you see that I have." And while they still disbelieved for joy, and wondered, he said to them, "Have you anything here to eat?" They gave him a piece of broiled fish, and he took it and ate before them.

Third step: asking the Lord for the grace I want:
Lord Jesus, give me the grace to know you better so that I can love you more and follow you more

closely. Help me to know you better as my consoler. Let me share in the gladness and the joy of your resurrection. Teach me to pray. Teach me to be with you in the peace and the gladness of your resurrection.

After the three preliminary steps, I should go as the Lord moves me in my prayer. I should do whatever I feel most comfortable doing with the risen Lord. I might remain quiet, contemplating the risen Jesus looking at me with love. Or I might want to make a prayerful reflection. Here are a few ideas.

Prayerful reflection:

Jesus, I hear you saying to me the same thing that you said to the apostles when you appeared to them in the upper room after your resurrection: "Why are you troubled, and why do questionings arise in your heart?" Yes, Lord Jesus, I believe your glorious presence here with me. I accept all the love that you have for me, the love of your risen and glorified heart. I accept the consolation of your loving me and being here with me.

Jesus, you are my hope and my consolation. I do not know what the future holds for me. But I do know that you hold my future in your hands. You are the Lord of the future by reason of your resurrection. I put into your hands all my worries and fears about the future. I am in your loving hands, Jesus. You are my future. You are my rock of hope. You are my consolation.

Lord Jesus, I feel secure in your love. You carry in your hands and feet and side the wounds you suffered for me, for my salvation, so that, risen, you could be with me now. I feel secure, Lord, in your faithful and generous love.

Contemplation.

Rest quietly in the Lord. You might want to repeat the name *Jesus* very slowly in your heart in order to center yourself on the risen Jesus present in your prayer. Or you might want to look at Jesus with love and sing to him quietly in tongues. Or perhaps you will quietly sing a simple hymn to him, for example, "You are Lord; you are Lord; you are risen from the dead and you are Lord; every knee . . . ," or some other hymn that you know well.

Let Jesus minister to you. Be quiet. No need for words or thoughts or ideas or even specific feelings. Just be there. Let Jesus do what he wants. Let him minister to you.

FOUR

Traditional Practices and Contemplation

A householder . . . brings out from his storeroom
things both new and old. (Mt 13:52)

T HE CHURCH IS THE HOUSEHOLDER, adapting to each
culture and to each age of the church. Some of
the traditional prayer practices of pre-Vatican II
days went back into store: for a while Benediction
seemed obsolete, Stations of the Cross found no
place in new churches or were taken away in the
liturgical orientation of older churches.

Now many of these practices are returning—
shorn of accretions and spontaneously rediscovered.

The wisdom and value of such traditional ways of
prayer as the rosary, the Stations of the Cross, and
exposition of the Blessed Sacrament is, first, that
they are suitable to all levels of our spiritual
development—from the beginner in prayer to the

most loving. Second, they are Scripture-based.

In this section we take some of these practices and see how we can use them to help us contemplate and come to know Jesus.

Contemplation and Fasting

A little experience soon makes it clear that contemplation and fasting go together. Each makes the other possible. This discovery should not surprise us, because Jesus grouped prayer and fasting together in a striking way, in two parallel sayings:

> When you pray, go to your private room and, when you have shut your door, pray to your Father who is in that secret place, and your Father who sees all that is done in secret will reward you. (Mt 6:6)

> When you fast, put oil on your head and wash your face, so that no one will know you are fasting except your Father who sees all that is done in secret; and your Father who sees all that is done in secret will reward you. (Mt 6:17-18)

Both prayer and fasting are indispensable, not optional, in the Christian life. Jesus did not say, "*If* you pray . . . ," "*If* you fast . . . ," but, "*When* you pray . . . , "*When* you fast . . ."

There is no doubt that when we pray with fasting, things happen. The gifts of God and his goodness are free, and abundantly available to us, not to be earned or deserved. But often God cannot get to us. Fasting puts us squarely before him, where he can reach us, grace us, use us. We are vulnerable to God, less sufficient to ourselves.

Prayer with fasting shows God how deeply we care about whatever is our intention—whether it be repentance or intercession. This is an earnest prayer which God honors. Jesus, Son of God though he was, did not attempt to begin his public mission without prolonged fasting.

Whatever length of time we plan for prayer and fasting is between us and our Father, as Jesus taught. The tradition of the church has been Wednesday and Friday. Jesus' disciples did not fast. When questioned as to the reason, Jesus explained that fasting was not appropriate in times of joy, but that when he was taken away they would fast (Mt 9:14-15). So the early church took up the practice. The *Didache,* an early Christian document, instructs: "You shall fast on Wednesday and Friday" (*Didache* 8:1).

Bede (circa 673-735) in his *History of the English Church and People*, speaking of St. Aidan (651), says "Many devout men and women of that day were inspired to follow his example, and adopted the practice of fasting until None (late afternoon) on Wednesdays and Fridays, except during the fifty days after Easter" (p. 148, Penguin 1970 edition).

Rosaries.

At first sight the rosary would seem to be the most vocal of prayers—"Hail Mary" 150 times! But the purpose is to contemplate Jesus in the saving mysteries of his life, death, and resurrection. A "mystery," in this sense, is an event with a depth of meaning into which we can enter.

We can ponder these mysteries with Mary, who "treasured all these things and pondered them in her heart" (Lk 2:19).

As an example of praying the rosary in a contemplative way, we could take again the Annunciation (Lk 1:26-38).

I (Robert Faricy) would contemplate the mystery in this way: I look at the scene with Mary my mother, now glorified and with Jesus in heaven, while I say the words of the rosary. I do not think about the words of the Our Father or the Hail Mary. I just say them without adverting directly to their meaning. Instead, I *look*. I look at the angel Gabriel appearing to Mary, speaking to her. I look at Mary saying yes to God's will. I marvel that God takes human form.

The words I say help me to avoid distractions. My mind occupies itself not with those words but with the scene, with the interior image that represents the mystery. I enter into the mystery—in this case, of the Annunciation—in a contemplative way, without thinking or conceptualizing, but just looking with love.

Others may have the same problem as I (Sister Lucy) in saying the Hail Marys and contemplating the mystery simultaneously: I cannot say the Hail Mary without thinking of its meaning. So I say one or two, slowly, and then I look at just one of the persons in the mystery—for example, at God our heavenly Father, who has waited for this moment from eternity and now, "when the fullness of time came,...sent his Son, born of a woman" (Gal 4:4). I rejoice with our Father's joy in this supreme moment of his prodigal love for us. I see his delight in his Son made flesh: "This is my Son, the Beloved" (Mt 3:17). Or I look with God our Father at Mary. I feel his love for her: "You are wholly beautiful, my love, and without a blemish" (Sg 4:7).

Or I look at Jesus: "His state was divine, yet he did not cling to his equality with God but emptied himself to assume the condition of a slave, and became as men are" (Phil 2:6). Why? I ask Jesus, ask him how he felt at that moment; he remembers. I ask him about his prayer to his Father, about Mary his refuge, about how he was thinking of me in that moment. I look and listen.

Or I look at Mary, the girl of Nazareth—"Can anything good come from that place?" (Jn 1:46). Mary remembers well: "She was deeply disturbed"—"Do not be afraid"—"The power of the Most High will cover you with its shadow" (Lk 1). And "the Word was made flesh" (Jn 1:14). I remain quiet; I look and listen.

Another contemplative rosary is the *Rosary of Jesus*, traditional in Croatia. It consists of the Creed, then the Our Father thirty-three times (in honor of the years of Our Lord's life), and seven times the "Glory Be to the Father." The mysteries are seven in number. It is arranged like this:

The Creed

1. How Jesus was born

a. Reflect on this. (If the rosary is prayed in a group, there can be spontaneous reflection and prayer.)

b. Pause in silence, opening your heart to this mystery.

c. Petition for the grace of this mystery according to the needs of the particular persons for whom you pray.

d. "Our Father . . ." five times (three after the last mystery).

e. "O Jesus, be our strength and protection."

f. Hymn (optional).

(Repeat a to f for each mystery.)

2. How Jesus had compassion for the poor, the sick, the sinner, the abandoned, the weary.

3. How Jesus was ready, disposed, and open to God.

4. How Jesus had great hope in his Father.

5. How Jesus was not just ready to, but did in fact, give his life.

6. How Jesus conquered and won.

7. How Jesus ascended to heaven and sent the Holy Spirit.

End with seven Glory Be's and total abandonment to God.

The Stations of the Cross.
The traditional Way of the Cross has no set prayers, so it is eminently a contemplative prayer. At each "station" or stopping place, one does just that: stop and watch, see what is going on, and ask Jesus to take you into his memory, his thoughts at that time. Ask Mary, "Show to me the blessed fruit of your womb, Jesus." Take each station slowly.

1. Jesus is condemned to death. "He had not done anything wrong, and there had been no perjury in his mouth" (1 Pt 2:22). "By force and by law he was taken; would anyone plead his cause?" (Is 53:8). As we contemplate Jesus here, we could make a petition for those undergoing the same unjust condemnation now "by force and by law."

2. Jesus receives his cross. "He went out, bearing his own cross" (Jn 19:17). "And yet ours were the sufferings he bore, ours the sorrows he carried" (Is 53:4). "The Lord has laid on him the iniquity of us all" (Is 53:6). See Jesus, speak to him from your heart. Can I help Jesus now, in anyone who is burdened?

3. Jesus falls. "It was the will of the Lord to bruise him: he has put him to grief" (Is 53:10). "To the weak I became weak, that I might win the weak" (1 Cor 9:22). Jesus, here I am, weak and bruised; I see you bruised for my sins.

4. Jesus meets his mother. "A sword will pierce through your own soul also" (Lk 2:35). "Who can rescue and comfort you, virgin daughter of Zion?

For huge as the sea is your affliction" (Lam 2:13). Mary—what my salvation has cost you and Jesus!

5. *Simon helps Jesus carry the cross.* "They seized on a man, Simon from Cyrene, who was coming in from the country, and made him shoulder the cross and carry it behind Jesus" (Lk 23:26). For a while I see Jesus relieved of his cross. This is a moment to praise God for any cross I am carrying, to ask to be relieved of it if it is an obstacle to my coming to him; a moment to see if I can relieve Jesus in the person of my neighbor—"Insofar as you did this to one of the least of these brothers of mine, you did it to me" (Mt 26:40).

6. *Veronica wipes Jesus' face.* "The crowds were appalled on seeing him—so disfigured did he look that he seemed no longer human" (Is 52:14). I gaze at Jesus, "the fairest of the sons of men" (Ps 45:2).

7. *Jesus falls a second time.* "We thought of him as someone punished, struck by God, and brought low" (Is 53:4). "Thou dost lay me in the dust of death" (Ps 22:15). I see Jesus in the dust of my repeated failures and sins. I see in him the dregs of our society—could I help him up in them?

8. *The women of Jerusalem mourn for Jesus.* "But Jesus turned to them and said, 'Daughters of Jerusalem, do not weep for me; weep rather for yourselves and for your children. . . . For if men use the green wood like this, what will happen when it is dry?'" (Lk 23:28, 31). The women see Jesus, as I do. Yet their sorrow must lead to repentance and

change. Their lives are dry wood: "They know nothing of the way of peace, there is no fear of God before their eyes" (Rom 3:17-18). As I look at Jesus I ask myself, how genuine, how radical, is my option for him?

9. Jesus falls a third time. "We are weak, as he was, but we shall live with him, through the power of God" (2 Cor 13:4). Contemplating the weakness and degradation of Jesus, "the Holy Strong One," I can reflect with St. Paul, "I am quite content with my weaknesses, and with insults, hardships, persecutions, and the agonies I go through for Christ's sake. For it is when I am weak that I am strong" (2 Cor 12:10). Jesus looks at me with compassion. He tells me that all his strength is available to me.

10. Jesus is stripped of his garments. "They shared out my clothing among them. They cast lots for my clothes" (Jn 19:24). I see Jesus: "From the sole of the foot even to the head, there is no soundness, but bruises and sores and bleeding wounds" (Is 1:6). I reflect that Jesus stripped himself of all things—his equality with God, his life—for my sake: "He was rich, but became poor for my sake, to make me rich out of his poverty" (see 2 Cor 8:9). Let me then not reject the spiritual riches which he won for me.

11. Jesus is nailed to the cross. "He was pierced through for our faults, crushed for our sins. On him lies a punishment that brings us peace, and through his wounds we are healed" (Is 53:5). I see Jesus even at that moment; he was "praying all the time for sinners" (Is 53:12). "Father, forgive them; they do not know what they are doing" (Lk 23:34). I accept this forgiveness.

12. Jesus dies on the cross. "He was torn away from the land of the living; for our faults struck down in death" (Is 53:8). "He was bearing our faults in his own body on the cross, so that we might die to our faults and live for holiness" (1 Pt 2:24). Looking at Jesus, I see him dying that I might live. I ask him what he thought in that moment. I commend to him my living and dying. If I am afraid of death, I reflect that "since all the children share the same blood and flesh, he too shared equally in it, so that by his death he could take away all the power of the devil, who had power over death, and set free all those who had been held in slavery all their lives by the fear of death" (Heb 2:14-15). Mary stood by the cross at the death of Jesus; she will stand by me at my death.

13. Jesus is taken down from the cross. "His soul's anguish over, he shall see the light and be content" (Is 53:11). "It is accomplished" (Jn 19:30). Jesus' anguish is over. He has accomplished my salvation. I see him dead, in Mary's arms. I ask her to share her thoughts with me.

14. Jesus is laid in the tomb. "They gave him a grave with the wicked, a tomb with the rich" (Is 53:9). But already "death is swallowed up in victory" (1 Cor 15:55). "For it was impossible for him to be held in its [death's] power" (Acts 2:24). I look at Jesus dead and recall his words: "Do not be afraid; it is I, the

First and the Last; I am the Living One, I was dead and now I am to live for ever and ever" (Rv 1:17).

Group Worship and Contemplation

The charismatic prayer group is a community that meets to praise and worship the Lord. Does that mean that there is no place for contemplative prayer? No, the charismatic prayer group is a school of contemplative prayer. During the praise at the beginning and throughout the meeting, during the sacred songs, our eyes are on the Lord. Singing in tongues we "utter mysteries in the Spirit" (see 1 Cor 14:2). Praise, tongues, silence—our prayer goes beyond our understanding, words fall short. "I will pray with the spirit" (1 Cor 14:15). "When we cannot choose words in order to pray properly, the Spirit himself expresses our plea in a way that could never be put into words, and God who knows everything in our hearts knows perfectly well what he means" (Rom 8:26-27). This is contemplative prayer. During the teaching and the prophecies, our ears listen to the speaker, but our eyes are fixed on Jesus.

Eucharistic adoration, especially exposition, is returning to many of our churches. This is group worship, usually silent. Sometimes a prayer group arranges to be there together. We can spend time with Jesus in the Blessed Sacrament, saying little, content to be with him, letting him minister to us.

To be in the presence of God, of Jesus in the Eucharist, to be there in faith, is a mind-stunning experience. If we were exposed to some radioactive substance, we would expect to be profoundly affected. To kneel in the presence of the living God—can it leave us unchanged?

Final Note to the Reader

The great virtue of a person of prayer is perseverance. Love, of course, remains basic; prayer is about receiving the Lord's love and somehow responding to his love. And humility is fundamental; the basis of all the virtues, it stands as the foundational lowliness and openness required for true prayer. But perseverance is paramount.

A lady once told me, "Stay till the end of the meeting; the world belongs to those who stay till the end of the meeting." Do not cut your prayer time short; stay till the end of your meeting with the Lord. And stay faithful every day, until your meetings with him in this world are over and you see him face-to-face.

Perseverance in personal daily prayer is the principal form that humility before God takes. It takes humility to plod through the darkness and the dryness that can endure in daily prayer. It takes humility to stay small, so small that I have no room in me for the discouragement that comes from pride. Pride will tell me, "You're *still* not a saint; you don't know how to pray; you're not perfect even yet. You're wasting your time; give up." Humility says,

"You're no saint, but you're doing what they did and you're going through what they went through. The Lord is here, not high up, where your pride wants to take you, but down low, where you really are, in your nothingness, yearning to fill it."

Perseverance in daily prayer is, for most of us, the principal form that loving the Lord takes. Fidelity spells love. Love means not leaving, not quitting, not giving up, trying again. Married people know this. It applies to prayer. Love means being there, putting in the time. I'm here, Lord.

If you want the Lord, really want him, and if you want him enough to spend time with him faithfully every day, then that is enough. You don't need a book; your book is Jesus. He's in the Gospels; he's in your heart.

Your wanting him is his gift to you. Thank you, Lord.